Artificial Intelligence Simplified

Understanding Basic Concepts

Authors:

Binto George
Gail Carmichael

Editors:

Susan S. Mathai
Andrew Carmichael

Publisher's Website:

www.cstrends.com

ISBN: 1944708006
ISBN-13: 978-1944708009

Library of Congress Control Number: **2015920904**

HOW TO USE THIS BOOK

Artificial Intelligence (AI) will impact our lives in more ways than we can imagine. This book is for anyone wanting to learn AI concepts without an in-depth prior knowledge in the field. You should be able to use this book if you have some basic background in data structures and algorithms.

The book introduces key AI concepts in an easy-to-read format with examples and illustrations. Our emphasis is to keep our explanations as simple as possible. We feel that a complex, overly mathematical textbook does not always serve the purpose of conveying basic AI concepts to most people.

If you are a professional and wish to learn AI without complexities, this book is for you. If you are a robotics enthusiast wanting to understand the broader aspects of AI, you may find this book useful. If you are taking a basic AI course and find the traditional AI textbooks intimidating, you may use this as a "bridge" book, or as an introductory textbook.

DISCLAIMER

Authors and publisher make no representations or warranties on accuracy or completeness with respect to the information provided in this book. No implied warranties of fitness or merchantability are made for specific purposes. No one is authorized to offer any expressed or implied warranties on our behalf. Always seek appropriate professional advice before using any information provided in this book. NEITHER AUTHORS NOR PUBLISHER WILL BE LIABLE FOR ANY LOSSES OR DAMAGES INCLUDING WITHOUT LIMITATION, INDIRECT OR CONSEQUENTIAL LOSS OR DAMAGE.

Product and company names mentioned in this book may be trademarks or registered trademarks of their respective holders. Their use or appearance does not imply any affiliation with or endorsement by them.

Table of Contents

1. INTRODUCTION

Objectives

- [ ] Introduce AI
- [ ] Explore applications of AI
- [ ] Discuss the organization of the book
- [ ] Describe the operating room scheduling problem
- [ ] Introduce the generate-and-test problem solving method

If you have ever checked the weather, snapped a picture with your smart phone, or even just searched for information online, you have used Artificial Intelligence (AI). Modern applications of AI range from computer games to self-driving cars. Financial institutions use AI for fraud monitoring, investment decisions support, credit risk assessment, data mining of customer behaviors, and economic forecasting. The military uses AI for target discrimination, missile defense shields, and robot steering.

In the coming years, applications of AI are likely to touch every walk of life. We created this book to help you understand some of the major concepts of AI to help you succeed in such an environment.

You probably won't become an AI expert, or even know every detail of the concepts we present. But you will get a sense of some of the central ideas in AI through a context you can relate to.

The original objective of AI was to create systems that perceive, think and act like humans (Winston, 1992). Years of research have shown us that this is a tougher proposition than originally anticipated. While a few researchers continue their work towards achieving this objective, most others work instead toward the objective of developing systems that perform as good as or better than humans in a focused area such as chess playing or disease diagnosis.

Researchers have tried many different methods to achieve AI. Some believe that symbolic systems hold the key to the AI. A few believe heuristic searchers are the way to go. Others think that expert systems can capture human intelligence. Some focus on recreating the human brain by simulating neurons in the brain. In this book, we explain some of these methods in the context of realistic applications.

1.1. Organization

In this book, we tackle several different problem areas that can be addressed with AI techniques. For example, AI can help job scheduling in both the manufacturing and service industries by automatically generating high quality schedules while considering various parameters and meeting potentially conflicting objectives. AI can help find driving directions from one location to another through a network of roads with real-time updates based on dynamic events such as detours, constructions and accidents. If you are traveling to a number of cities and you want to return after visiting all cities exactly once, which route is the best for you? Questions like that can be solved using the search methods described in Chapter 2.

Planning is the process of deciding the sequence of actions to be performed for reaching one of the goal states starting from the current state. Planning helps us deal with surprise events that occur during otherwise normal course of operations. We can apply planning techniques to such domains as logistics, military campaigns, space exploration, and operating procedure synthesis. Chapter 3 explains planning.

There is an interesting AI method used for gaming, cryptographic code breaking, freight routing, data packet routing, market prediction, hardware design, signal filtering and signal processing. Genetic algorithms have origins in evolutionary biology, in which organisms evolve and adapt to thrive in environmental conditions. Learn more about genetic algorithms and evolutionary computing in Chapter 4.

Learning from experience is a sign of intelligence. Neural networks simulate the learning capacity of biological neurons in our brain. Neural networks can be effectively used for gesture recognition, speech recognition, handwriting recognition, fraud detection, cancer cell detection and petroleum exploration, and much more. In particular, big data systems handle huge volume and variety of data moved at extremely high speeds, where conventional data processing methods are not sufficient. Neural networks can predict patterns or devise processing strategies to sufficiently deal with big data. See Chapter 5 for more information on neural networks.

Expert systems can assist or even replace human experts with specialized knowledge. Expert systems for disease diagnosis include MYCIN (Shortliffe, 1977) and PUFF (Aikins, Kunz, Shortliffe, & Fallat, 1983). Expert systems can also be used as diagnostic tools for automobiles, airplanes and machinery. LITHIAN, an expert system, provides guidance to archeologists for exploring stone tools. DENDRAL (Lindsay, Feigenbaum, Buchanan, & Lederberg, 1980) is used for the identification of the structure of chemical compounds. Expert systems may also be used in auditing, taxation and accounting. One type of expert system, called a fuzzy expert system, is used for avoiding automobile collisions, auto-piloting airplanes, controlling Unmanned Area Vehicle (UAV), detecting cancer, diagnosing heart disease, evaluating insurance fraud, and predicting credit risk. See how expert systems work in Chapter 6.

In 1999, Deep Blue (Hsu, 2002), a computer program, won a chess game with then world chess master Garry Kasparov. The chess program used a special type of search called game tree search. Other board games can also be implemented using game trees. Game trees can also be used for devising a winning strategy weighing in conflicting options. Learn more about game trees in Chapter 7.

Jennings and Rutter are two highly regarded Jeopardy! (a TV quiz show) players. They lost to IBM's Watson, a computer, in a landmark Jeopardy! game in 2011 (Brown, 2012). Microsoft researchers developed an artificial humor system called CAHOOTS (Wen, Baym, Tamuz, Teevan, Dumais, & Kalai, 2015) that observes chat sessions and suggest funny pictures for users to respond with. Neither project would be possible without ensuring that computers can understand how we speak in everyday conversation. Digital assistants such as Siri®, Alexa™, Cortana™ can also interact with us using natural language. Chapter 8 describes how we can implement natural language processing on a computer.

What is the benchmark of intelligence? Is it obtaining a human level IQ score? Is it showing a human level performance in a specific area, such as disease diagnosis or chess playing? Or is it the ability of a computer to convincingly mimic a human being? Chapter 9 explains the classic test of artificial intelligence.

What is super-intelligence (Bostrom, 2014)? Under what circumstances the super intelligence can be dangerous? Can computers take over the planet? Chapter 10 summarizes the developments in AI and explore future directions. The chapter also discusses issues such as ethical AI (Anderson & Anderson, 2007).

To make AI more accessible to you, we have chosen to present key AI concepts in a context that everyone can relate to. We focus on two important healthcare applications: operating room (ORoom) scheduling and computer-aided diagnosis.

1.2. The Operating Room Scheduling Problem

The scheduling problem appears in many areas, including healthcare (Zweben & Fox, 1994; Gomes, 2000; Cardoen, Demeulemeester, & Beliën, 2010). A hospital's operating room provides a prime example: surgeries must be scheduled according to several rules and considerations. For example, the availability of surgeons, anesthesiologists, nurses, equipment, medicine, and operating rooms must be taken into account. Some rules are mandatory for patient safety, while others are desirable for patient comfort and hospital profitability.

With many (potentially conflicting) requirements on a surgery schedule, how can we quickly and easily find one that works?

Let's consider what an AI-based scheduling system might look like for a hospital with two operating rooms. Please note that actual scheduling systems are complex (Zweben & Fox, 1994; Cardoen,

Demeulemeester, & Beliën, 2010) and what we present here is a much simplified version to help you to understand basic AI concepts.

Assume the system needs to support the following requirements:

Requirement 1: Surgeons want the operating rooms (ORoom1 and ORoom2) to be available for procedures whenever the need arises. This scenario is described with two blank rectangles indicating that the ORooms are available all the time (Figure 1-1).

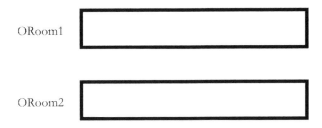

Figure 1-1: Surgeon's preference.

Requirement 2: Administrators want the operating rooms to be fully utilized, illustrated by two filled rectangles (Figure 1-2). This preference is understandable because scheduling one additional case per day can result in substantial revenue per year.

Figure 1-2: Administrator's preference.

Requirement 3: Anesthesiologists like procedures to start intermittently (Figure 1-3). This way they can start a procedure with one patient while monitoring another patient who is in post-operative recovery.

Figure 1-3: Anesthesiologist's preference.

Requirement 4: Staffers would like a predictable schedule with clear start and end times as well as breaks (Figure 1-4). They also want to avoid having to stay late during the day.

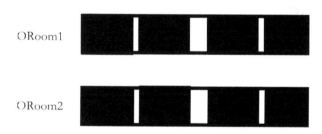

Figure 1-4: Staffer's preference.

It looks impossible for a schedule to meet all of the above requirements. For instance, Requirement 1 and Requirement 2 cannot possibly be fulfilled at the same time. However, if we look at the desires behind the requirements, it may be possible for a scheduler to simultaneously achieve both. How?

Surgeons do not actually want ORooms to be completely empty all of the time; they just want to be able to schedule elective procedures without unreasonable delays. Likewise, the hospital's administration does not actually want the ORooms to be at full capacity at all times, as that would introduce a high level of risk; they just want to maximize the ORoom's use by scheduling surgeries as efficiently as possible.

Based on insights like these, we can come up with a more realistic set of rules for our scheduler:

Rule 1: Patient wait-times for surgeries should be minimized.

Rule 2: ORoom utilization should be maximized.

Rule 3: Procedure start times between the two ORooms should be staggered by a minimum of 20 minutes.

Rule 4: The difference between the staff's daily schedule and the actual schedule followed should be minimized. The lunch hour will ideally be between 12:00pm and 1:00pm, and no elective surgeries should be performed before 7:00am or after 6:30pm.

Now that we have a reasonable set of rules, we must somehow use them to come up with the best possible schedule for our ORooms.

1.3. Generate and Test

A simple approach to solving the scheduling problem is to generate schedules and test to see if the schedules satisfy our rules (Russell & Norvig, 2009). As seen in Figure 1-5, the general idea is to come up with a possible schedule, check whether it satisfies the rules, and continue generating new schedules until one of them passes the test.

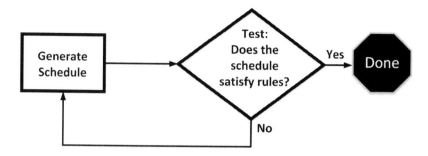

Figure 1-5: Generate and test.

A simplified schedule created by the generator might look something like the one shown in Figure 1-6.

Schedule				
Slot No	O Room #	Surgery Start Time	Expected Surgery Duration	Patient Name
1	1	7:00am	120 min	Linda
2	2	7:20am	105 min	Bill
3	1	9:20am	170 min	Matt
4	2	9:25am	165 min	Warren
5	1	12:30pm	190 min	Phil
6	2	1:30pm	150 min	Sue
7	2	4:20pm	130 min	John
8	1	5:00pm	90 min	Jenna

Figure 1-6: Example schedule for two operating rooms.

There may also be a waiting list for those yet to be scheduled, as shown in Figure 1-7.

Waiting List				
Slot No	O Room #	Surgery Start Time	Expected Surgery Duration	Patient Name
			60 min	Peter
			240 min	Ram

Figure 1-7: Waiting list for those yet to be scheduled.

Try sketching the schedule in a more visual form, and check whether Rule 3 has been met. That is, are the procedure start times staggered by a minimum of 20 minutes?

You have just tested a generated schedule against one of the rules. A scheduling system would continue to test the other three rules to see if the candidate schedule is acceptable.

How many different schedules are we going to have to generate and test? Suppose the candidate schedule above is not acceptable. If this happens, another schedule would be generated and tested. In some cases, we don't know whether we have generated the right schedule just by looking at it. For instance, we don't know if the patient wait-time has been minimized unless we explore other schedules or somehow determine that we cannot improve the wait time any further. So it seems that there could be a huge number of possible schedules to try before finding one that works.

Consider the problem of scheduling ten patients into two ORooms. Disregarding procedure start times, how many different ways could these ten patients be scheduled?

Imagine there are ten slots into which patients can be scheduled. In Slot 1, any of the 10 patients could be scheduled. For slot 2, we can pick one of the remaining 9 patients. For slot 3, any of the remaining 8 patients could be scheduled, and so on. Continuing this pattern, the total number of potential combinations would be $10 \times 9 \times 8 \times 7 \times 6 \times 5 \times 4 \times 3 \times 2 \times 1 = 10! = 3{,}628{,}800$ different schedules!

If we assume that a hospital typically performs 40 surgeries a day, there would be $40! = 8.1591528 \times 10^{47}$ potential schedules. And that's without even considering varying start times.

Clearly, we need our system to be intelligent about generating new candidate schedules. Picking random schedules until we find one that works would simply take too long (Cheeseman, Kanefsky, & Taylor, 1991). We'll have a look at one way to systematically find the schedule we're looking for in the next chapter.

2. SCHEDULING WITH SEARCH METHODS

Objectives

- ☐ See how data structures are used for problem solving
- ☐ Understand blind searches and their limitations
- ☐ Understand how heuristics can be used to improve search
- ☐ Learn the basics of heuristic search algorithms and their limitations
- ☐ Introduce best path methods

In the previous chapter, we learned about the scheduling problem in AI, and discussed how we might use computers to schedule procedures in a hospital operating room. Here, we'll see how we can intelligently structure our search for a schedule that fits our criteria.

One way to approach finding a good schedule is to imagine intelligently working through an interconnected network of related candidate schedules until one that satisfies our rules is found. This is known as **state space search**.

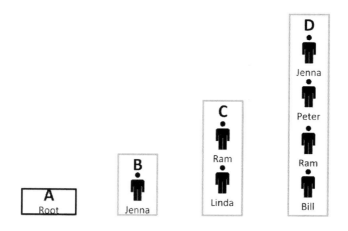

Figure 2-1: Example schedules as nodes.

For the ORoom scheduling problem, we would think of states as schedules with zero or more slots filled in with a procedure. For example, Figure 2-1 shows four different states: the first (A) represents an empty schedule, the second (B) a schedule with one slot filled in with patients, the third (C) a schedule with two slots filled in with patients and the fourth (D) a schedule with four slots filled in with patients.

We can represent relationships between schedules using something called a **tree**. In computer science, trees are data structures that are similar to the concept of a family tree. Formally, a tree contains a set of **nodes**, each of which represents one entity (for example, a single person in a family tree). A node in a tree can have a number of **children** (just like people can have children in family trees), but only one **parent**. A node is connected to its parent and children with **edges**. The root of the tree is a special node with no parent. We often imagine the root being the 'top' of the tree.

(Please see the next page for a schedule tree.)

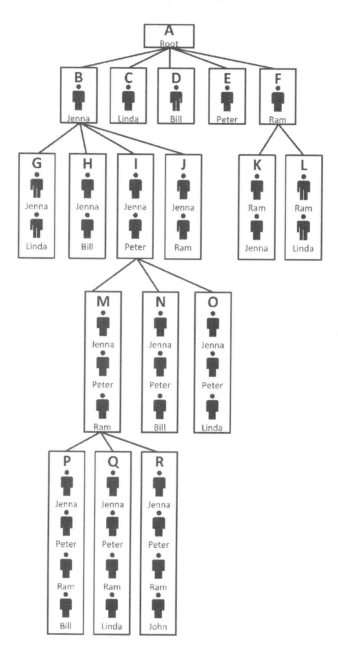

Figure 2-2: A partial example of a surgery schedule tree. Starting from an empty root node, more patients are added into the schedule as we go down the tree.

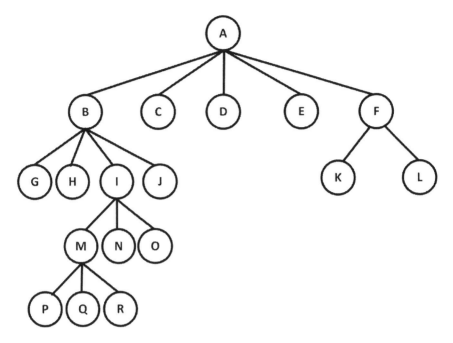

Figure 2-3: Simplified tree representation of the schedule in Figure 2-2.

In our schedule tree, each node represents one schedule. The root of the tree will be a node representing the empty schedule. The children of nodes will contain a new schedule that has exactly one more patient added to a surgery slot than their parents have. A portion of one possible schedule tree is shown in Figure 2-2. A simplified representation of the same tree is shown in Figure 2-3.

If we are careful to include all possible schedules for a particular set of patients and ORoom slots, we can use our tree to find a schedule that satisfies all of our rules. If such a schedule exists, that must be part of the tree somewhere. In general, a tree that organizes various states of what we are searching for is called a **state space tree**.

2.1. Blind Search Methods

Blind search (Cormen, Leiserson, Rivest, & Stein, 2009) involves exhaustively looking through all nodes in the search space until we find the schedule that best satisfies all of our rules. Blind searching is very inefficient (Aho, Hopcroft, & Ullman, 1974) because we are not using any domain-specific knowledge to be smart about how we search.

Figure 2-4: Blind searching is like trying to get to the peak without using knowledge of the mountain's geography; you would be hoping to find the peak by chance.

Blind searching is only useful when the size of the tree is relatively small. With a huge tree, searching for a goal state is like climbing to the peak of Mount Everest with a blindfold on (Figure 2-4) – in-fact, climbing Mount Everest may turn out to be easier!

We can search the tree randomly or in a systematic way (Knuth D. E., 1973). For example, with the depth-first search (DFS) technique, we check nodes by working our way down a tree until the bottom-most node on a branch is reached. If we need to keep searching, we backtrack a step and work down other branches.

In the example search tree shown in Figure 2-5, suppose we are searching for the node labeled N. A depth-first search would begin its search at the root, A. It would continue to B and then to F, which is the bottom-most node in that branch. Since F is still not the node we are looking for, the search tries to continue, but F has no children. So the search closes the node F and backtracks to B, then continues down the next branch to G. The search continues in this fashion, eventually reaching the goal N.

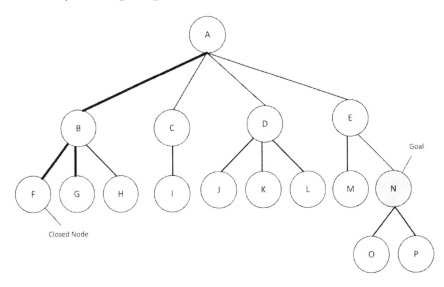

Figure 2-5: An example of searching for node N in a tree using depth-first search.

Breadth-first search (BFS) (Aho, Hopcroft, & Ullman, 1974) is another example of a blind searching method where the search proceeds level by level. In the above example, the search would start at root node A and explore the neighboring nodes B, C, D, and E first. Since the search doesn't find the goal, the search expands to the next level of neighbors F, G, H, I, J, K, L, M and N. Finally, the search stops when it finds the goal, N.

With any blind searching strategy, we are not making use of any available knowledge to direct our search to where the goal schedule is likely to be found. As a result, we have to look at every node (i.e., every ORoom schedule) in our search space. However, if we could use a numerical value to indicate how suitable an ORoom schedule is, we might be able to find our goal faster. That's what we describe in the next section.

2.2. Heuristic Search Methods

So far in this chapter, we have talked about blind searches in the context of scheduling a hospital operating room. We saw that blind searching methods could help us find a schedule that fits all of our scheduling criteria, but quickly realized how infeasible doing so would be when the number of possible schedules is huge.

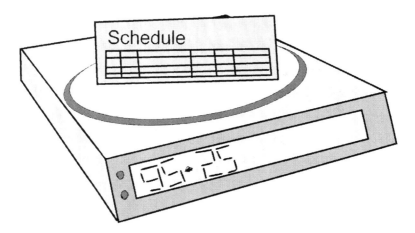

Figure 2-6: Heuristics are a measure of quality.

Suppose that we had access to some kind of device (Figure 2-6) that measures how 'good' a schedule is, even if the schedule is only partially filled in. We could use such a device when building a schedule from scratch to see if the next change we make produces a better schedule, or a worse one. This way, we can avoid clearly bad choices. Such a device is called a **heuristic function** and can be used to improve our search.

Designing a heuristic function that can satisfy all requirements for surgery scheduling is a complex task (Blazewicz, Lenstra, & Kan, 1981). As a simple example, consider what a heuristic function might look like for just one of our rules. How could we use a number to reflect the quality of a schedule with respect to the requirement of maximizing ORoom usage?

If we are trying to maximize the ORoom utilization, a simple approach is to make the heuristic function return the total amount of time that procedures in the schedule take. We give the heuristic function a schedule, and it returns a number. The larger the number is, the better.

Assume that we have designed a heuristic function incorporating all of our scheduling rules. The higher the number given to us by the function, the better the schedule is overall. We can use our heuristic function to know whether a new assignment to a procedure slot is likely to make a better schedule or not.

For instance, assume the heuristic function's result for the current partial schedule is 360. If the next slot assignment results in a value of 270, we are going away from the goal. On the other hand, if the slot assignment results in a value of 400, we are getting closer to the goal.

Having a heuristic function does not make finding a goal state trivial. The heuristics are, at best, estimates. We also need to use heuristics wisely as we search for the best schedule, as we will see in the next few sections.

With a heuristic function in our toolbox, we can refine our state space searching technique to perform a more intelligent search (Kanal & Kumar, 1988; Nilsson N. J., Problem-solving methods in Artificial Intelligence, 1971; Pearl, 1984, Simon & Newell, 1958;

Slagle, 1971). Instead of systematically searching each branch of a tree as in depth-first search, we'll choose where to search next based on heuristic knowledge of the schedules in the tree.

2.2.1 Hill Climbing

Hill climbing is a search algorithm that makes use of heuristic values. It involves following a path in the tree that is based on how the current heuristic value changes relative to the value associated with the next node in the path.

When we use **simple hill climbing**, we follow the *first* path we find that improves the heuristic value. In contrast, with **steepest ascent hill climbing**, we look at all paths and pick the *best* one from our current position.

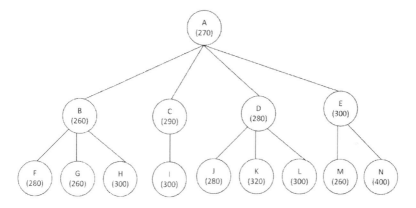

Figure 2-7: A tree representing different nodes labeled A through N, each with a heuristic value shown in parentheses.

Suppose the tree shown in Figure 2-7 represents possible ORoom schedules as in previous sections. We want to find the best schedule in the tree using hill climbing. We would begin at the root, then check the next schedules among the root's children (say, left to right), checking which ones improve the heuristic value.

Trace through the tree in Figure 2-7 and see if you can list the nodes we would examine if we were to use simple hill climbing, and whether the list would be different if we used steepest ascent hill climbing.

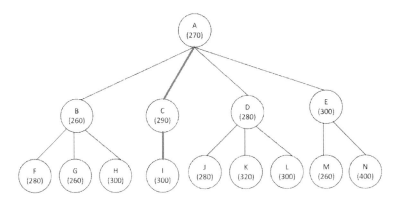

Figure 2-8: The path taken when simple hill climbing is used.

Figure 2-8 shows the path taken when simple hill climbing is used. In this case, the first promising path is always taken, whether or not there is a more promising path to be found later on. The heuristic value of node A is 270. The search doesn't go through B, because it appears less promising with a smaller heuristic value than the current node. The search goes through C and then finally to I.

Steepest ascent hill climbing takes the best path available, as in Figure 2-9. Node E has the highest heuristic value after node A. Therefore, the search proceeds through E and ends on N.

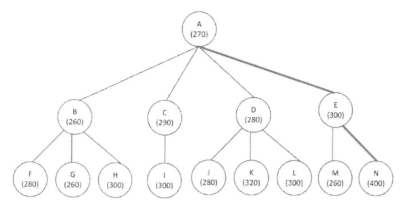

Figure 2-9: The path taken when steepest ascent hill climbing is used.

You may have noticed in our example that we only needed to check one path through the search tree. Compare that with depth-first search and other blind techniques that required us to check many or even all paths. It certainly seems that hill climbing is the way to go, but it is not without its limitations.

Limitations of Hill Climbing

Hill climbing seems to help us find the best ORoom schedule quite efficiently. However, in some cases, the technique can lead us astray. As we try to climb the mountain of ever increasing heuristic values, we always go for the steepest (i.e., best) path currently available to us. This is known as a **greedy approach** and can cause us to get stuck with a state that appears to be the best from where we're standing, but isn't really the best overall.

Consider the tree in Figure 2-10. If we use steepest ascent hill climbing, we will follow the path from node A to E to N. From N, the best of the only two choices is O, but since its heuristic value is smaller than N's, we stop at N and declare the schedule at node N to be the best. Unfortunately, we completely missed out on finding node L, the true goal of the search, because node E looked more promising than node D.

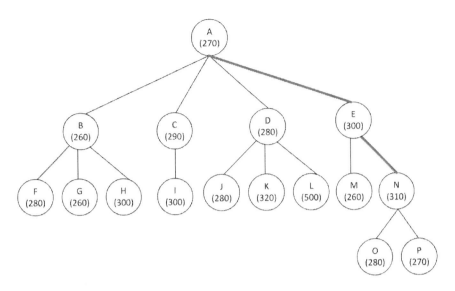

Figure 2-10: A hill climbing example that ends on a foothill (local maxima).

Figure 2-11: The hiker following a hill climbing algorithm reaches a foothill.

The example in Figure 2-10 illustrates the search algorithm getting stuck on something like a foothill (formally called a **local maxima**). Although one path might be steeper than another, the gentler ascent might eventually lead to a higher peak that we'd never know about after taking the steeper path (see Figure 2-11).

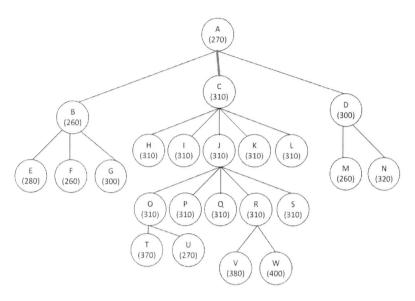

Figure 2-12: A hill climbing example that results in being stuck on a plateau at node C.

Figure 2-13: The hiker does not know which direction will lead to the peak, as all the ground around him is at the same height.

Figure 2-12 shows a different problem. How would you perform steepest ascent hill climbing search on that tree? The search proceeds up to node C, at which point we do not know which path to take, since all heuristic values are the same (310). The search will have to work harder here by exploring numerous paths until it gets to the goal at node W. This situation is called a **plateau**, and can make the hill climbing process take longer (see Figure 2-13).

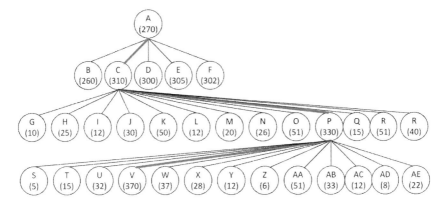

Figure 2-14: A hill climbing example illustrating a ridge.

Finally, consider Figure 2-14. Here, the search finds itself on a **ridge** when it reaches node C. In general, very few paths go upwards from a ridge toward to the goal; most paths take the search substantially downwards. As a result, the search needs to examine a large number of paths just to make sure that it does not miss the few paths that exist to the goal.

Figure 2-15: The hiker finds it hard to follow the path that goes up as many paths go sharply down.

Again the search slows down, as seen in Figure 2-15, where the hiker finds himself on a ridge trying to climb through the sharp edge.

Despite these limitations (Konolige, 1994), hill climbing does help find the goal much faster than blind searches in most scenarios. It is also possible to overcome these limitations by adding to the search strategy.

The hill climbing search can also follow a **simulated annealing** schedule (Russell & Norvig, 2009), where the search takes higher risk in the beginning by choosing more paths randomly. The search is likely to explore paths that appear less promising because those paths may still have some potential to be the best choice later. As the search progresses, the search behaves increasingly like hill climbing. Simulated annealing reduces (but does not eliminate) the chance of being stuck on a foothill.

If the search stops at a foothill before reaching the goal node, a hill climbing algorithm with a restart mechanism can still help us to find the goal by backtracking from the foothill and continuing. Even still, the search can keep climbing back to the foothill. With restart, the search eventually reaches the goal after potentially restarting several times, but the restarts can diminish the efficiency of hill climbing.

2.2.2 Best First Search

One of the reasons we run into limitations with hill climbing is that we take the most promising path as soon as we see it, disregarding the possibility that other paths might ultimately lead us to better results. The **best first search** approach overcomes this by remembering all partial paths taken during the search. The search can continue from any of the partial paths if the current path becomes less promising. The downside of this approach is that it uses a lot of memory storage to remember all partial paths.

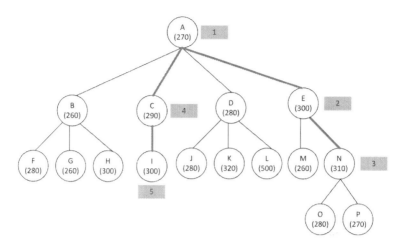

Figure 2-16: An example of a best first search, where the edge labels in rectangles indicate the order paths were taken in.

Figure 2-16 shows an example of best first search. The search starts at root node, A, adding its children into a list prioritized based on their heuristic values. Of the nodes in the list, at first, node E looks like the most promising choice based on the heuristic value. So the search expands node E adding M and N into the list. At this point, N is the best node in the list. So the search expands N adding the children O and P also into the list. The heuristic values are low for nodes O and P. So instead of going further down that path, the search expands the best node in the list, which is C. As a result, the search tries the path from A to C to I. The search continues in this way until we reach the goal node L. See if you can find out how the search proceeds from I, which is not shown in the figure.

2.3. Best Path Methods

For some applications, multiple paths exist to the goal. We are usually interested in finding the best path as well as the goal. For example, we might want to not only find a way for an ambulance to arrive at the emergency room, but we want to ensure they get there as fast as possible (Moore, 1959; Dreyfus S. E., 1969). For this type of scenario, we need to use a **best path search**.

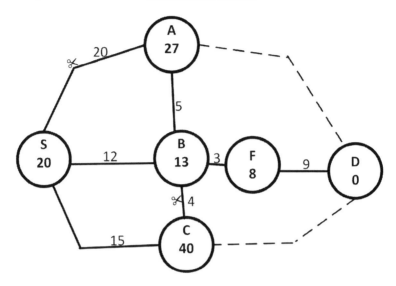

Figure 2-17: Example of an A* search from the source S to the destination D.

One popular best path method is called **A*** (pronounced "A star") (Dechter & Pearl, 1985). Similar to best first search, it expands from the most promising node seen so far. The heuristic used in A* is the sum of the actual distance traveled to the current node and the estimated remaining distance to the destination. The best path is the path that minimizes the heuristic value. An A* search stops when it reaches the destination, and does not continue exploring. At any point, if we happen to overestimate the remaining distance, A* may not find the best path.

Figure 2-17 shows an A* search in progress. In the context of an ambulance finding the best route, the nodes represent street intersections while edges represent roadways connecting the nodes. The number shown inside the node is the estimated remaining distance to the destination. For example, B is estimated to be 13 units away from the destination. What is the estimated distance from F? In this case, 8 units. The number shown against an edge is the actual distance observed when traversing that edge. For instance, the edge SC has an actual distance of 15 units. The distance for edge FD is 9 units.

The thick lines show the paths already explored by the end of the following description:

The search begins at source S and tries to find destination D. From S, the search calculates the heuristic values to the neighbors, i.e., for paths SA $(20 + 27 = 47)$, SB $(12 + 13 = 25)$, and SC $(15 + 40 = 55)$. Note heuristic value is the sum of actual distance travelled and estimated remaining distance to the destination. Of the paths, the heuristic value for SB is the smallest, so the search will continue from there.

From the path SB, the search calculates the heuristic values to the neighbors, which are, SBA $(12 + 5 + 27 = 44)$, SBF $(12 + 3 + 8 = 23)$, SBC $(12 + 4 + 40 = 56)$. Notice that the sum of the total distance travelled to reach the last node on the path so far (that is, A, F, and C) includes the actual distance from S to B as well as from B to the new node.

We can reach C directly from S with an actual distance of 15 units (path SC). From S, we can also reach C through B (path SBC) with an actual distance of 16 units. That means SC is better than SBC. So the SBC will be deleted based on the **dynamic programming principle** that essentially says, for a complete path to be the best, all its partial paths should be the best as well. With the same logic, SA is deleted in favor of SBA. Deleted paths are marked in Figure 2-17.

Of the remaining paths, SB, SC, SBA, and SBF the heuristic value for SBF is the smallest, so the search will continue from there.

The destination D is the only place to go at this point, and so the search concludes with a best path of SBFD.

In summary, blind methods search through the space without using any intelligence. Their downside is their efficiency. Heuristic methods, on the other hand, make use of the available information to direct the search more intelligently for reaching the goal faster. Although almost all our examples in this chapter are on trees, search methods can also work on more complex data structures such as graphs, in which multiple edges may enter a node or there can even be cyclical paths. However, if the search is interested only in finding a node, the optimal search path will still be a tree. Why?

Many search methods we found in this chapter are interested only in locating the goal node, but not in finding the best path. Best path methods such as A* find the best path from a given source to the destination.

In some situations, it will be more efficient to dynamically determine the problem solving strategy rather than using one of the search methods described above. In those cases, a problem solving strategy can be planned in advance by specifying the possible actions and their pre-conditions. When the required pre-conditions are satisfied, the system can determine the actions to be performed for progressing towards the goal and then execute those actions. We discuss this further in the next chapter.

3. ACCOMMODATING SURPRISES WITH PLANNING TECHNIQUES

Objectives

- ☐ Introduce planning
- ☐ Understand different types of planning, including:
- ☐   forward,
- ☐   backward,
- ☐   and partial order planning
- ☐ See how to plan under uncertainty

Even with a good schedule, surprises can happen. For example, during a surgical procedure a backup roller pump might need to be arranged, or equipment may be switched from another console. What if a surgery requires additional personnel? Or if an unforeseen emergency procedure must be scheduled? Not only do we need to adjust our schedule to accommodate the new procedures or equipment disruptions, but we also want to get back on track with our previously scheduled procedures as soon as possible. Planning techniques can help us do just that.

Planning (Wilensky, 1983; LaValle, 2006) is the process of moving from a **start state** to a **goal state** by applying a series of **actions**. In our example, the start state is the schedule we were working with before an interruption occurs. The goal state is a schedule that both accommodates any required changes (such as new emergency procedures) and includes procedures that were originally planned. The goal state should also incorporate the requirements we saw in the introduction. We need to figure out how to get from the start state to a goal state, possibly without knowing what the goal state is.

At any stage between the start and end states, actions change the current state in some way. For example, we can have an action called 'bump' that will remove a patient from the surgery schedule. An emergency procedure can be added to the ORoom schedule after bumping the procedure originally scheduled to start next. However, the bumped procedure may not be able to wait until the next day, or it cannot go through the normal surgery scheduling process. In this case, we need another action called 'add' to add a procedure back to the ORoom schedule. Additional rules may also be required to keep disruptions to a minimum, such as ensuring urgent procedures or pediatric cases are not bumped, or that safety requirements are not violated.

There are multiple approaches to solving the planning problem; we discuss a few of these next.

3.1. Forward Planning

The simplest approach to planning is called **forward planning** (also known as **progression planning**). In this approach, we start with known start states and apply actions until we get to a goal state.

When we have to accommodate an emergency procedure, our current schedule is an undesirable state, shown as the *source* in Figure 3-1 (on the next page). New schedules that effectively accommodate both the emergency and existing procedures are the *desirable goals*, labeled D1 through D4. These schedules can be described by a set of constraints or specifically picked out manually by the ORoom scheduling nurse as one of the desirable outcomes. The actions *add* (+) or *bump* (-) can make the state change from the source to an intermediate state such as A, B, F, or E.

In some cases, a threat may block the transition between states. For example, in order to proceed from one schedule state to another, certain equipment needs to be available for the procedure being added. If the equipment is unavailable, the planning process is blocked.

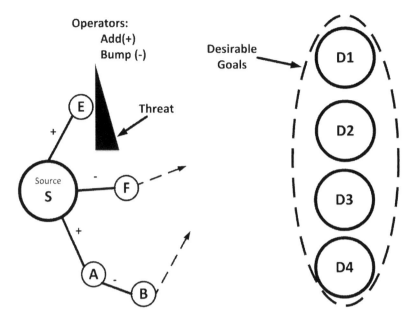

Figure 3-1: A high-level view of the planning process. Our goal is to find a series of actions that take us from the source, an undesirable state, to one of the destinations, or desirable goals.

3.2. Backward Planning

In contrast to forward planning, **backward planning** (or **regression planning**) starts from the goals and backtracks to reach the start state. Doing so allows us to focus on the most relevant actions, whereas a forward search can branch out in many directions and won't even necessarily reach one of the goals.

We can only use backward planning when the goals are clearly specified. If the scheduling nurse can pinpoint some goal schedules, then backward planning makes sense. If no specific goals are known, but we have a number of constraints to identify goal states, we cannot use backward planning and need to choose something else.

3.3. Partial-Order Planning

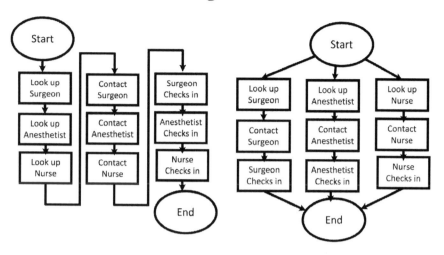

Figure 3-2: Dividing a plan (left) into sub-plans (right) offers more flexibility.

In forward and backward planning, we have a plan and we start either from start states or goal states. However, there are situations where dividing a plan into sub-plans offers more flexibility.

For instance, adding an emergency surgery into a schedule involves ensuring surgeon availability, equipment availability, and staff availability. We can have one sub-plan for finding surgeons, another sub-plan for obtaining necessary equipment, and another sub-plan for checking the availability of the nursing staff. We call this type of planning **partial order planning**.

Figure 3-2 shows an example plan on the left, and how the same plan could be divided into sub-plans on the right. In the original plan, the anesthetist needs to wait until the surgeon checks in. However, in the subdivided plan, each individual plan can be executed independently, providing more flexibility in the ordering of the individual actions.

Developing heuristics for partial order planning is difficult as it is hard to know what impact executing a sub-plan will have on the overall goal. Suppose, for example, we had two sub-plans: one for finding surgeons, and another for finding support staff. Imagine that the heuristic for selecting a staffer is his or her earliest availability time. Executing these two sub-plans may result in a surgical team that has never worked together as a team before, which may not work the best for the overall goal. However, calling the surgeon first might have helped us select a nurse who has worked with that surgeon before.

3.4. Planning Under Uncertainty

In the above cases we assumed that we will always be certain about what state we are in. In the real world scenarios, this may not always be the case – we also need to be able to plan when we don't exactly know what state we're in (Etzioni, Hanks, Weld, Draper, Lesh, & Williamson, 1992).

For instance, suppose we have called the surgeon, but he has not yet checked in. He could be on his way, but we can't be sure. What should we do? We could go to an earlier state and try to schedule another surgeon, or we could wait a few minutes to see if the surgeon arrives after all. In order to make a better choice, we can attempt to increase our confidence in our understanding of the scenario, for example by checking whether the receptionist saw the surgeon walk in.

In the discussion in the previous sections, we assumed that an action will make a transition from one state to the other. In real life, the effect of an action is actually not certain either. Instead of knowing exactly what outcome will occur when we apply an action, we need to be able to work with a probability that an action will produce a particular outcome.

In addition to our current state and the outcome of an action, the goal can be uncertain as well. For example, there could be competing objectives. However, even if we cannot guarantee that we will reach a goal, we can get closer to it by considering various beliefs about the environment and working with trade-offs. For example, we might move forward by trying to minimize worst-case scenarios (such as patient death) and then try to improve the patient satisfaction (such as reduction of pain).

Whatever the approach to planning or the level of uncertainty, planning techniques help us decide ahead of time what actions to perform to achieve certain objectives. When the planning is complete, we will have a complete plan that either meets given constraints or declares failure.

In our example, planning helps us accommodate the emergency procedure and get back on the existing schedule with minimal disruption. We may also use the search methods described in the previous chapter to generate a totally new schedule, but that might cause many patient slot assignments to be rearranged, which may not be convenient.

So far we have explored how we can generate optimal ORoom schedules by using various search methods. We also learned how planning can accommodate emergency procedures into already existing ORoom schedule. In the next chapter, we will explore a novel way of evolving schedules without searching at all.

4. EVOLVING SCHEDULES WITH GENETIC ALGORITHMS

Objectives

- ☐ Introduce the idea of evolutionary computing
- ☐ See how genetic algorithms can solve the scheduling problem
- ☐ Explain the reproduction cycle (selection, mutation and crossover)
- ☐ Introduce basics of genetic programming

In the search techniques discussed so far, we traversed the search space in various ways to try and find the best schedule as quickly as possible. As we saw, searches can sometimes be inefficient, and we can get stuck in local maxima (see Section 2.2.1). These issues can be avoided if we keep track of information about the paths we have traversed, but doing so requires more space in memory.

Genetic algorithms (GAs) (Baum, Boneh, & Garrett, 1995) provide an alternate approach to creating an ORoom schedule that simulates an evolutionary process. GAs work by combining two parent chromosomes to produce something new in the offspring. If we are careful to allow only the fittest to survive, we may end up with a very good set of chromosomes—and therefore a good solution to the state space search—after a large number of generations are produced.

In the ORoom scheduling context, we say that a chromosome is a set of schedule slot assignments. Each slot assignment represents a gene. When the genetic algorithm starts, we create a set of randomly generated chromosomes (schedules). These act as our first generation that we will evolve over many iterations.

Encoding schedules into genes (Davis L. , 1985) and setting up a GA system for finding the best schedules is more complex than we can describe here. For our purposes, assume that we can schedule exactly five surgeries per day and there are eight patients waiting for surgery. The patients are assigned numerical identifiers from 1 to 8. We want to use a GA to find out which combination of five patients would give us the best schedule. We start by generating four initial schedules randomly as shown in Figure 4-1.

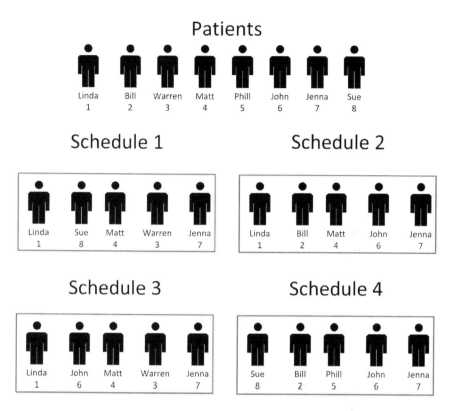

Figure 4-1: Initial surgery schedules created from the pool of patients.

For each new generation of chromosomes, a **fitness function** is used to choose the best chromosomes in a process called **selection**. A fitness function is a lot like a heuristic function: while a heuristic function helps us reach the best solution, a fitness function tells us *how good* a solution is. In our example, suppose that Schedule 1 and Schedule 4 are the fittest chromosomes; these are the schedules chosen to participate in the next generation.

Once we have selected the best schedules in the last generation, we modify them using two processes.

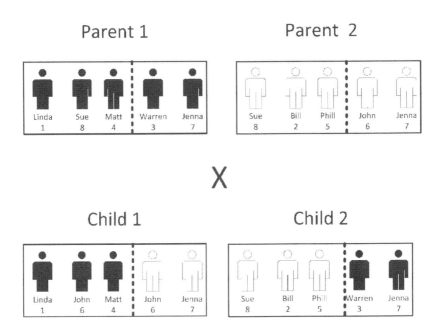

Figure 4-2: Two schedules are modified using crossover.

The first process is called **crossover**, which we perform with a predefined probability (as a result, it may not happen at all). A crossover swaps genes between two chromosomes to produce new ones. For schedules, that means some of the slot assignments are traded, as shown in Figure 4-2. The shading in the figure helps us see where the genes in the children came from. The dotted line shows the crossover point, where the chromosomes are broken apart and genes are exchanged. The crossover point may be chosen randomly.

Figure 4-3: One schedule is changed through mutation.

The second process is called **mutation**, which we again apply with a probability. Mutation affects a chromosome by randomly choosing a gene to alter in a random way. This means a single schedule slot assignment will be randomly changed, as shown in Figure 4-3, where John is replaced with Bill. The mutation may introduce interesting properties that parents never had.

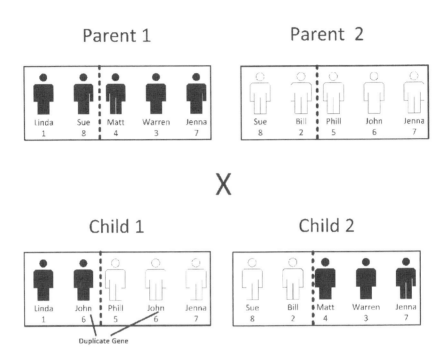

Figure 4-4: An example of a defective schedule where John is scheduled twice.

Crossover and mutation don't always go smoothly, as illustrated in Figure 4-4. If a crossover happens at the dotted line, we will end up with a defective chromosome (Child 1) because John is scheduled twice. To help combat this issue, genetic algorithms have mechanisms to detect defective chromosomes and repair or regenerate them.

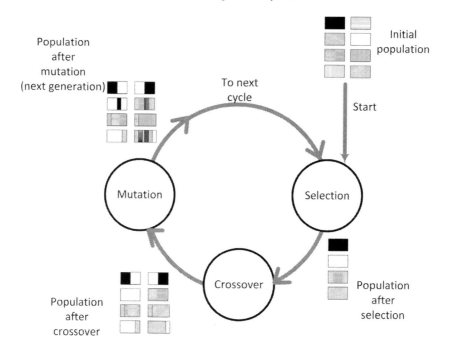

Figure 4-5: Overview of the reproduction cycle in genetic algorithms.

Figure 4-5 summarizes the evolutionary process of creating a new generation of schedules from the old generation by selection, crossover and mutation. If no mutation or crossover happens within one reproduction cycle, the parents will be added to the candidate pool for the next generation. Ideally, however, there will be some change after each generation; some research focuses on ensuring there is diversity among chromosomes in a population (Nsakanda, Price, Diaby, & Graveld, April 2007). The evolutionary process continues until we find a satisfactory solution or for a specified number of generations.

4.1. Genetic Programming

We can apply GA principles to automatically evolve computer programs from a population of random programs (Koza, 1992; Banzhaf, Francone, Keller, & Nordin, 1998; Langdon & Poli, 2002).

For example, suppose we want to automatically evolve a computer program that performs ORoom scheduling. The genetic programming process can start with an initial generation of random programs. In our case, the fitness score of each program can be computed based on how well the program's outputs match with manually developed benchmark schedules. Programs earning better fitness scores can be selected to participate in the next generation. The selected programs then undergo crossover and mutation resulting in the next generation of programs. The evolution process can continue until we have a program that can reliably schedule surgical procedures.

How does an evolved program that solves our scheduling problem actually work? We don't know. It may be using best first search, a genetic algorithm, hill climbing or combination of all methods. Theoretically, we could reverse engineer the program to find out.

Besides solving scheduling problems, genetic programming can automatically generate programs for detecting malignant tumors from radiograms (Worzel, Yub, Almal, & Chinnaiyan, February 2009). Genetic programming has also been successful in demonstrating human-level performance in several areas (Koza, Keane, Yu, Bennet III, & Mydlowec, 2000).

According to the theory of modern evolutionary synthesis, all species, including human beings, evolved after several reproduction cycles spanned over millions of years. We consider ourselves the most intelligent creature on the planet. Our intelligence is attributed to our brains' several billion interconnected neurons. Can we create AI by simulating our own brains? We explore that in the next chapter.

5. LEARNING FROM EXPERIENCE WITH NEURAL NETWORKS

Objectives

- ☐ Understand the structure of a neuron
- ☐ See how neural networks can solve simple problems
- ☐ Introduce multi-layer neural networks with hidden layers
- ☐ Understand the concept of supervised and unsupervised learning

The methods we have used so far to generate schedules have not taken into account what actually happens at an individual hospital. For example, not every surgeon performs a procedure at the same speed. It would be useful to be able to adjust the scheduling process to take this into account. We need a scheduling system that can learn from experience and improve itself.

Learning from experience is something the human brain does quite naturally. We can use **Artificial Neural Networks (ANNs)** (Haykin, 1998; Anthony & Bartlett, 2009; Cowan & Sharp, 1988) to simulate the network of hundreds of billions of neurons found in the brain. A single neuron, shown in Figure 5-1, is connected to hundreds of other neurons that feed in inputs (stimuli). A neural network can be set up to represent complex logic, and we can even have a neural network learn logic on its own.

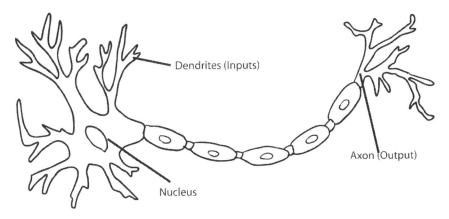

Figure 5-1: A single neuron (shown above) that would be connected to hundreds of others in a neural network.

A real neuron can be quite complex, so we will work with the simple model of a neuron shown in Figure 5-2. This model has an aggregate module and an activation function, both explained next.

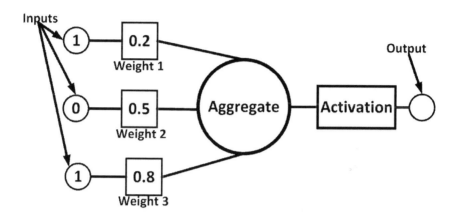

Figure 5-2: A simple model of an artificial neuron.

Aggregate Module

In Figure 5-2, there are three inputs. Each input is weighted by values shown in rectangles. Weights can be positive or negative. The **aggregate module** adds up all weighted inputs. The output of the aggregate module in the diagram is $1 * 0.2 + 0 * 0.5 + 1 * 0.8 = 1.0$.

Activation Function

The **activation function** determines the output of the neuron. The step function, illustrated in Figure 5-3, is one of the most commonly used activation functions.

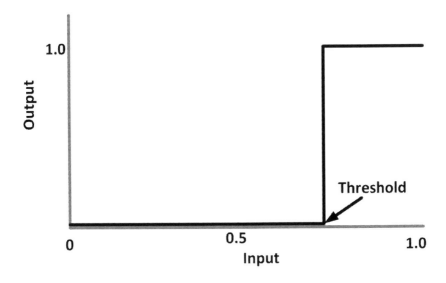

Figure 5-3: Step activation function.

The x-axis shows the input of the function ranging from 0 to 1, and the y-axis shows the output of the function. At a threshold point in the input, the output jumps (that is, steps) from 0 to 1. The step function simulates the firing of a biological neuron. When the sum of the inputs is below the threshold, the neuron is not fired (i.,e., the output is 0). When the neuron gets enough stimulation that the sum of the inputs becomes above the threshold, the neuron fires (generating an output of 1), and the output is passed on to other neurons connected to it.

What would the output be for the neuron in our example if the inputs are 1, 0, and 1? The output of the aggregate module is 1, which is clearly above the threshold. Therefore the neuron is fired and its output will be 1. If the inputs were 0, 0, and 0, however, the output of the aggregate module would also be 0. This would not be enough to fire the neuron, so the output of the neuron ends up being 0.

Let's see how an ANN can learn with an example. Suppose that a particular kind of surgery would be prolonged if there is a new person on the surgical team or a patient is high risk. How does the neuron learn this logic? Once we have an ANN for the problem at hand, we can train neurons to produce a certain output. Suppose our ANN has only one neuron. The learning happens by adjusting the weights. Figure 5-4 summarizes what the outputs of a neuron should be given particular combinations of inputs.

New Team Member (Input 1)	Patient is High Risk (Input 2)	Prolonged Surgery (Desired Output)
0	0	0
0	1	1
1	0	1
1	1	1

Figure 5-4: A description of the inputs for the scenario of prolonged surgeries, and the desired output in those cases.

We can train the two input neurons to learn this logic by adjusting their weights. Assume that we are using a step activation function with a threshold of 0.5 and that both weights are 0.25. Now we can test to see if the neuron has learned the above logic, as summarized in Figure 5-5 (on the next page).

Input 1	Input 2	Input 1 x Weight 1	Input 2 x Weight 2	Total	Actual Output
0	0	0	0	0	0 ☑
0	1	0	0.25	0.25	0 ☒
1	0	0.25	0	0.25	0 ☒
1	1	0.25	0.25	0.5	1 ☑

Figure 5-5: Summary of tests applied to a neuron with a threshold of 0.5 and weights of 0.25.

Our test reveals that two of the four outputs were correct. We continue training the neuron by adjusting the weights in various combinations until all the outputs are correct. When both weights are 0.5, the neuron will produce the correct output for all input combinations, as shown in Figure 5-6.

Input 1	Input 2	Input 1 x Weight 1	Input 2 x Weight 2	Total	Actual Output
0	0	0	0	0	0 ☑
0	1	0	0.5	0.5	1 ☑
1	0	0.5	0	0.5	1 ☑
1	1	0.5	0.5	1.0	1 ☑

Figure 5-6: Summary of tests applied to a neuron with a threshold of 0.5 and weights of 0.5.

When we find a combination of weights that produce the desired output, we say that the neuron has learned.

5.1. Multi-layer neural networks

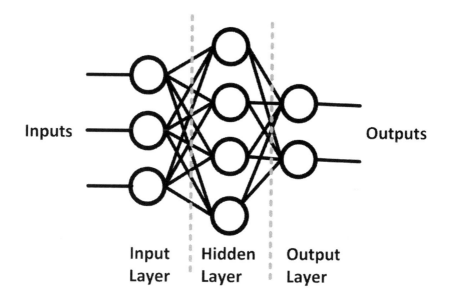

Inputs

Outputs

Input
Layer

Hidden
Layer

Output
Layer

Figure 5-7: Multi-layer ANN

A single neuron cannot learn very complex logic. (Can you can train a single neuron to learn 'exclusive-or, also written as XOR, logic? See Appendix B for details.)

We can construct and train a more complex ANN with many neurons using the same ideas as in our simple example. Figure 5-7 shows an ANN with multiple layers. Such an ANN is capable of 'deep learning' (Schmidhuber, 2015) problem solving strategies for tackling real-life challenges. It's worth noting that simply adding more neurons to a network does not necessarily result in better learning. This is because a network with a large number of neurons can result in the network memorizing facts rather than generalizing them (Baum & Haussler, 1989).

How do you train a multi-layer ANN? In one multi-layer ANN popular for training (Rumelhart, Hinton, & Williams, 1986), called a back propagation network, the error is first computed for a sample input set as the difference between the expected output and the observed output. If the error is at an unacceptable level, the training continues by adjusting the weights contributing to the error. The weight adjustments are made layer by layer starting at the output layer, propagating backwards through the hidden layers and ending at the input layer.

The weight adjustment factor is often computed as the error multiplied by the **learning rate**. The learning rate determines the manner in which ANN learns. If the learning rate is set high, the ANN tries to learn quickly but sometimes may not learn very well or at all. If the learning rate is set low, the ANN learns slowly, but there is a higher chance of completing the learning successfully.

If we want to solve the scheduling problem with an ANN (Johnston & Adorf, 1992), we can train the ANN with a good training set of surgeries and corresponding schedules. The ANN learns correlations between inputs and outputs from the presented data. For example, a particular surgeon might always be assigned to afternoon slots, perhaps because she prefers to avoid early mornings. The ANN may learn this pattern from training schedules and try to assign afternoon slots for that surgeon.

Once we train the ANN (Swingler, 1996), we can test it with a never-before-presented set of surgery orders. Testing and training continues until we get satisfactory results.

The downside of using an ANN is that we are not sure why an ANN is performing the way it is, or whether it will perform consistently under all circumstances. While this makes ANNs seem unreliable, the situation is not very different from, say, a driver passing a road test and getting a driver's license. There is no guarantee that he or she will be accident free later on.

Everything we have discussed in this chapter so far is known as **supervised learning** (Kröse & van der Smagt, 1993): an ANN is trained and tested with sample input-output data sets. Interestingly, an ANN can also perform **unsupervised learning** (Kohonen, 2000) by coming up with its own observations from the presented inputs. Unsupervised learning works well for applications in data classification, such as finding tumors by spotting anomalies in tissue analysis (Menéndez, de Cos Juez, Lasheras, & Álvarez, 2010).

So far in this book, we have seen how AI can generate ORoom schedules using heuristic searchers and genetic algorithms. We have also seen how ANN can learn from experience and generate schedules tailored for a specific hospital environment. In the next chapter, we will see how AI can handle another important problem: medical diagnosis.

6. EXPERT SYSTEMS FOR DIAGNOSIS

Objectives

- Understand how a simple expert system works
- Define expert system types
- Understand how fuzzy logic can capture real life situations
- Learn about fuzzy expert systems

Doctors use their knowledge to diagnose patient problems, usually by asking a series of questions about symptoms to narrow down possible causes. A computer system that stores more information than a person could hope to remember is a very helpful addition to the process (Gorry, 1973).

A diagnosis system might store a set of if-then rules. For example, a simple rule might be:

If the body temperature is *greater than* 100.5 degrees,

then the patient has a fever.

A follow-up rule might be:

If a patient has a fever,

then administer acetaminophen as per the doctor's advice.

A system that can mimic the way people make decisions is called an **expert system** (Jackson, 1998). An overview of what an expert system is made up of is shown in Figure 6-1.

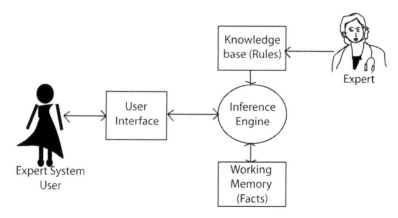

Figure 6-1: Components of an expert system.

When setting up a particular expert system (Ullman, 1989; Rolston, 1988), domain experts add rules into the **knowledge base**. Once the system is ready to use, users of the system can enter facts into the **working memory**. For a doctor, this might be information like the patient's temperature. The expert system then uses the **inference engine** to find rules that the facts happen to satisfy, resolving conflicts using a predefined strategy. When a single rule is chosen, the results of the rule are added to the working memory and the process continues.

For example, suppose our expert system has the rules above as well as this one:

> *If* amount of acetaminophen administered is *greater than* the maximum allowed limit per day,
>
> *then* do not administer any more acetaminophen, but call the doctor.

If a child's fever indicates that acetaminophen is to be given but the dosage indicates that it should not, the conflict resolution strategy will pick which rule will be applied. In this case, it should be that acetaminophen is not administered.

6.1. Expert System Types

Depending on how an expert system performs inference, there are many types.

6.1.1 Forward chaining

Say we have the following rules. First, Rule 1:

> *If* the patient has fever, runny nose, inflamed eyes and enlarged lymph nodes
>
> *then* the patient has rubella.

Rule 2:

> *If* the patient has fever, body ache, loss of appetite, tiredness and rashes,

> *then* the patient has chickenpox.

A **forward chaining** expert system collects all facts and sees which rule can be satisfied (i.e., triggered). Imagine that a patient complains of fever, body ache, loss of appetite, tiredness, runny nose and rashes. Rule 1 does not trigger since the patient has no inflamed eyes or enlarged lymph nodes. What about Rule 2? Yes, Rule 2 applies. The expert system infers that the patient has chickenpox and adds this new fact to the working memory. The inference process continues until no new facts can be added.

The disadvantage of forward chaining is that we may not always know what facts are relevant for solving the problem. The forward chaining is helpful if we are reasonably sure about the facts to be collected and the expert system quickly converges to a particular result.

6.1.2 Backward chaining

Backward chaining is useful when we have a limited, clearly defined set of facts (goals) to prove or disprove. The expert system starts from the goals and works backwards. In our example, the system might start from right hand side of the Rule 1 (the patient has rubella). In order to prove that the patient has rubella, the system should prove that patients has the following symptoms: fever, runny nose, inflamed red eyes, enlarged lymph nodes. The system checks to see if the patient has those symptoms and determines the following: fever, yes; runny nose, yes; inflamed red eyes, no; enlarged lymph nodes, no. Since the patient doesn't have inflamed eyes and enlarged lymph nodes, the system cannot prove the goal (rubella).

Now the expert system sees if it can prove whether the patient has chickenpox. Symptoms for chickenpox are: fever, body ache, loss of appetite and tiredness. The expert system already knows that the patient has a fever from the previous interaction, so it explores if the patient has any of the other symptoms: body ache, loss of appetite, tiredness and rashes. In our case, the answer is yes to all symptoms. The system concludes that the patient has chickenpox.

For backward chaining to work, the patient doesn't have to mention all symptoms in the beginning of the process. The system can ask for additional information as it is needed while working on proving or disproving goals. Also, the system enables us to collect only relevant facts: information such as the patient having read a book yesterday or talked to her parents don't have anything to do with the diagnosis.

6.1.3 Hybrid chaining

In some cases, the combination of backward and forward chaining is helpful. We call this **hybrid chaining**. The system starts with some initial facts and then goes forward to deduce new facts. For instance, the patient may state that she has a fever, runny nose, and inflamed red eyes. The system can shortlist potential diseases associated with those symptoms. Then the system can narrow in on a particular disease by ruling out or ruling in one disease after another on the list. During the process, the system might ask for additional information to prove or disprove a goal. For example, for rubella, it might ask, "Does the patient have enlarged lymph nodes?" since this fact is not in the working memory.

6.1.4 Deduction and reaction systems

In cases we have seen so far, the system comes up with a diagnosis by applying rules and adding new facts into the working memory. We call such systems **deduction systems**.

On the other hand, if we may develop a system that can administer medicines or summon a surgeon if the required conditions are met. We want such a system to be able to make inferences and act on them. We call these systems **reaction systems**.

In a deduction system, if we accidently add incorrect facts, we can simply retract and continue the inference. Retractions in reaction system could be difficult or even impossible, however, since some actions may be irreversible.

6.2. Fuzzy Expert Systems

Imagine that a stroke risk assessment expert system has the following rule:

If age is *greater than* 70,

then risk is present.

We can rewrite the rule more formally as follows:

R1: if age > 70
    risk = true

The boundary for this rule is rather strict: if you are 70 or under you are ok, but if you are even a day older than 70, you have a stroke risk. In reality, there is no such sharp boundary separating low and high risk. Instead we know that 'older' people have a higher risk than 'younger' people for some interpretation of older and younger.

What exactly do we mean by 'older'? Some may consider 50 years as old while others may consider 60 or 70 as old. (The young at heart might even argue that no age is old!) Despite the ambiguity, we do know that considering 70 years as old is truer than saying 50 is old. In other words, we have degrees of truth. Many facts behave this way, and do not have a crisp line between true and false.

Instead of defining truth as binary, we can represent the degree of truth as a number varying between 0 and 1, determined by what is called a **membership function**. Given an input, the membership function returns the membership value that quantifies the degree of truth.

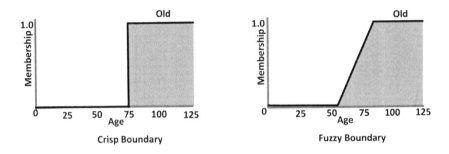

Figure 6-2: A comparison of sharp and fuzzy boundaries for age.

Figure 6-2 illustrates membership values for 'oldness.' The x-axis shows a person's age, and the y-axis shows the degree to which the age belongs to a particular membership category with young at the bottom (0) and old at the top (1).

When using a crisp boundary, anyone 70 or above is considered old. If someone is even one second younger than 70, then she is not considered old. Crisp boundaries are what we normally find when working with conventional logic.

If we instead use a fuzzy boundary (Zadeh, 1965; Zimmermann, 1991), the degree of truth increases as age goes up from 50 to 75, as shown in Figure 6-2. Someone who is 50 is old with a degree of truth 0 – in other words, they are considered young. Someone who is 75 is old with a degree of truth 1.0. A 70 year old is also old, but with lesser degree of truth: just 0.8.

Defining the rules with fuzzy boundaries and performing fuzzy inference can be useful for many real-life applications ranging from cancer detection to autopiloting aircraft. Please see Appendix C for more information on fuzzy expert systems and the fuzzy inference process.

Expert systems can also be useful for games. A player can consult an expert system to get advice on the best move. Expert system can also help coaches to come up with player defense or attacks.

The next chapter talks about a special kind of search useful in multi-player board games. The same search method can also be used for weighing in business options to win over the competition.

7. HANDLING COMPETING GOALS WITH GAME TREES

Objectives

- ☐ Learn how to model adversarial objectives
- ☐ Understand basics of min-max search
- ☐ Understand methods for improving efficiency - alpha beta pruning
- ☐ See how to search under time constraints and discuss progressive deepening and its effect on search

The problems we have seen in the book so far have had a single goal or set of goals that satisfy a single objective. For example, we wanted to find the best schedule, or find a diagnosis given a set of symptoms. However, there are instances where multiple possibilities compete against each other. If a patient has a particular condition, is it better treated with medicine, or surgery? What steps should a hospital take to compete with another hospital? Should you reduce treatment costs or get new equipment? What if the other hospital does the same? Then what? There are a number of real-life applications where role-playing, much like in multi-player games, can help us make better decisions. We can model adversarial dynamics with a new kind of tree called a **game tree** (also known more formally as a **min-max tree**) (Beal D. F., 1980).

Suppose that two hospitals in the area are competing with each other. Imagine that we have designed a heuristic function that is a quality measure of a specific position in their game. Our heuristic will represent how advantageous the position is for each hospital and can be measured as the difference of their revenues or number of patients treated.

Using the new heuristic function, we can perform a state-space search to find a winning position. Consider the example game tree in Figure 7-1 (on the next page). Recall that leaf nodes are the nodes with no children. A white leaf node means that Hospital A wins, while a black leaf node means that Hospital B wins. A grey leaf node indicates a draw.

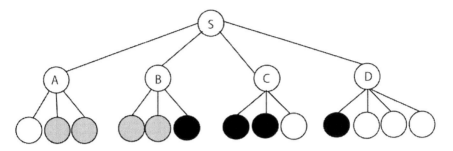

Figure 7-1: An example game tree.

Suppose we design a heuristic function that returns the difference between the number of white and black leaf nodes for a given branch. This heuristic function makes sense because a player wants to make a move that is more advantageous to them and less advantageous to the opponent.

One hospital is trying to maximize the heuristic value, so we call them the **maximizer**. The other hospital is looking to minimize the heuristic value, so we call them the **minimizer**. Although in real life hospitals can act whenever they want, for simplicity, we assume they take turns. (This is actually not a bad assumption because a hospital is more likely to act directly in response to what the competition does.)

Assume the maximizer gets to act first. If we use steepest-ascent hill climbing, the search would start at S, likely proceed to the game position represented by node D, and attempt to reach one of the white leaf nodes. Unfortunately, this approach would not work since the hospitals take turns. So the maximizer can only change his position once before minimizer gets to move.

Imagine that the maximizer moves to D. On the minimizer's turn, the minimizer can easily choose the black leaf node from D and thus win the game. Therefore, it is better for maximizer to move to A. This way, minimizer will be forced into a draw. We assume that both hospital administrations are equally competent, and always select the best option available to them.

Using a game tree, is it possible to understand the game's positions well enough to plan the best possible move to make each turn? The answer is to think ahead: if I make this move, what will my opponent do in response? Assuming they do that, what will I do next? We can continue exploring moves alternating maximization and minimization until time runs out, or until we have a clear strategy to win. For more information on the min-max search algorithm, please see Russel and Norvig (2009).

Alpha-Beta Pruning

Alpha-beta pruning (Knuth & Moore, 1975) is a technique used to reduce the number of game positions we need to search in a game tree. The idea is based on the principle that if we know a potential path is clearly worse than the best path we already know, we really don't need to learn how bad it is. We can simply avoid that path.

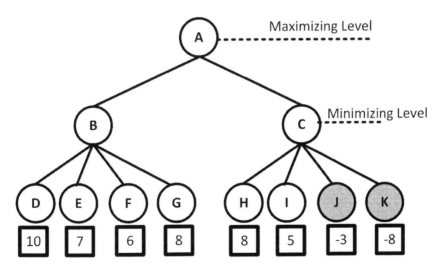

Figure 7-2: Alpha-beta pruning.

We explain alpha-beta pruning with the help of Figure 7-2. Assume that the maximizer plays first. He searches the tree to see which of the two options is best for him (in the diagram, B or C). He considers option B, but knows that the minimizer has the next turn. So the maximizer puts himself in minimizer's shoes to see which option the minimizer will pick from nodes D through G. The minimizer will pick the lowest heuristic score: 6. So if the maximizer plays B, a score of 6 is the best outcome he can achieve.

Next, the maximizer considers option C to see if he can get a score better than 6. When he explores node H, it has a score 8, which is better than the score 6. So he continues the search hoping that all nodes in that branch will be 8 or better. If that turns out to be the case, the minimizer will be forced to choose 8. That is a better deal for maximizer, but that needs to be verified.

The search expands to I, but the score here is only 5. The maximizer knows that the minimizer will prefer 5 over 8, so if the maximizer plays option C the best score he can hope for is at most 5. Since the maximizer can get a score of 6 by playing B, he doesn't want to explore option C any further. As a result, J and K are pruned from the tree and never searched.

Search Time Limit

In many situations, a move must be made within a certain time-frame. Searching the whole tree will take a very long time. So our search is limited to a fixed number of levels. We may not get the best answer with the limited search, but that is the best we can do.

Terminating searches early may lead to a **horizon effect**. Danger may lurk beneath what you can see, like a deer waiting to jump just beyond the reach of your headlights while driving at night. The solution: although the search is supposed to terminate at a pre-determined level, look deeper when you observe turbulent changes in heuristic values potentially warning of the trouble ahead.

Progressive Deepening

What if we finish our search early and there is some time left? We can deepen our search to one additional level. If we have time to finish our new search, we may have a better answer. If time runs out while the new search is in progress, we can play based on the previous search results. This technique is called **progressive deepening** or **iterative deepening**. While progressive deepening can improve the quality of results to a certain extent, after a few levels there may not be significant quality improvement (Nau, 1980).

We have seen how search can capture the adversarial dynamics of a multi-player games or business competition. We also learned techniques to limit the search and come up with the best possible results within the available timeframe. We saw that the horizon effect can cripple the search along with strategies for avoiding the horizon effect. All of this helps computers play games or strategize like we intelligent human beings do.

There is something that people naturally do, but that is very challenging for even the most sophisticated computer: the ability to understand each other in a conversation in our native language. If understanding natural language is a sign of intelligence, how can we get computers to do that? That is the focus of the next chapter.

8. COMMUNICATING WITH NATURAL LANGUAGE

Objectives

- ☐ Understand how chatbots work
- ☐ Explore natural language understanding (NLU)
- ☐ Provide a brief overview of research in NLU

In the previous chapters, we looked at how to automatically create an operating room schedule and use a computer to support diagnosis. We are restricted in how we interact with systems accomplishing these tasks according to the user interfaces they provide. Designing effective interfaces is difficult; there is a whole field dedicated to just that! Instead of trying to get the interface just right, what if we could just talk to the system instead?

When we have a conversation with another person, we are using what is called **natural language**. The rules that govern whether the things we say can be understood are very complex. As a result, it is difficult to program a computer to understand and respond to us in a general and believable way (Jurafsky & Martin, 2000; Church, 2003).

A **chatbot** is an example of a program that attempts to communicate with us in natural language. You can try talking to one called Alice (Schumaker & Chen, 2010) at http://alice.pandorabots.com/. What kinds of things can Alice respond logically to? How long does it take to realize that your conversation partner is definitely not human?

How does Alice work? Alice's 'brain' contains a number of modules called categories telling how to respond to user inputs. Each category includes an input pattern and one or more associated response templates. When you type something, Alice tries to find a match with the stored input patterns. On finding a match, Alice responds with the response template associated with that input pattern.

Categories

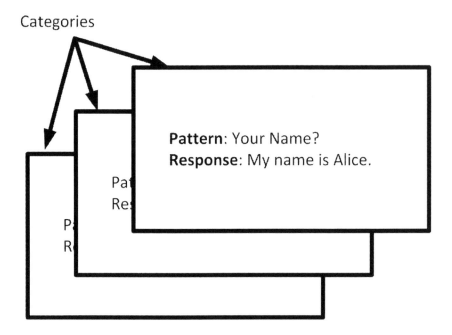

Figure 8-1: Alice's brain contains a number of categories. Each category has a pattern and response template.

As shown in example Figure 8-1, when you say, "Your Name?" Alice searches for a category that has a pattern matching your input. After finding the category, Alice responds as specified in that category: "My name is Alice."

Alice does not really understand the conversation, but merely responds as she is programmed to do. How can we use a chatbot like Alice to schedule a surgery or interact with an expert system? Although the chatbot doesn't know how to do these things, we can define categories to match patterns of speech that we'd expect to hear. For example, if the user says, "I would like to schedule a surgery," the response template might say, "Patient's name, please."

Of course, the same thing can be asked in many ways. For example, to schedule a surgery, we might say, "I need to schedule this surgery," or we might say, "May I schedule a surgery?" In order to handle this, a technique called **symbolic reduction** is used to map different articulations of the same concept to a single category, such as "Schedule Surgery," as illustrated in Figure 8-2.

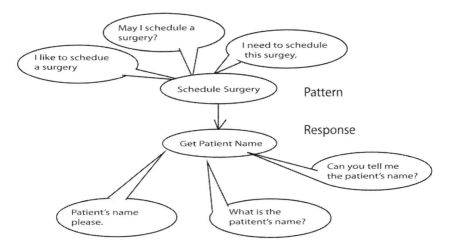

Figure 8-2: How symbolic reduction works.

After our request has been located, we expect a natural response in return. To avoid giving the exact same response every time somebody asks to schedule a surgery, our chatbot can randomize how the next request is phrased (Livingstone, 2006).

In some cases Alice may not be able to locate what we are asking for. To address this problem, there are default categories. For instance, if the input does not match with any of the built-in categories, we can set the response as, "I am sorry, I didn't understand. Please say that again."

8.1. Natural Language Understanding

It probably didn't take you very long to notice that Alice doesn't actually understand conversations you have with her. She just responds in a predetermined manner. If we used a similar chatbot in our own systems, our users might feel frustrated, or the process could lead to inaccuracy in scheduling or diagnosis.

Real conversations tend to cover a broad range of knowledge. For example, a doctor might ask for information about a particular medical condition, or a radiologist may dictate a report to the computer. Either of these people could just as easily casually ask about a baseball game's score. The computer has to precisely understand the question and should answer quickly with a high degree of accuracy.

Natural Language Understanding (NLU) (Winograd, 1972; Allen, 1995) works in three steps, as shown in Figure 8-3. The first step involves **syntax analysis**, which determines the linguistic structure of a sentence and the grammatical role each word plays in the sentence. The next step is to generate the **semantic interpretation** (i.e., meaning) of what the user said. Finally, the semantic interpretation is integrated to **contextual and world knowledge interpretation** to form an expanded semantic interpretation, as explained below. We need this last step because the meaning depends on the context, and often the proper understanding of a sentence requires world knowledge.

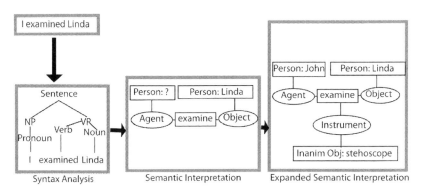

Figure 8-3: The three steps of natural language understanding.

82

Consider the sentence in Figure 8-3: "I examined Linda." In the first step of natural language understanding, the syntactic analysis will parse the sentence into a noun phrase (NP) and verb phrase (VP) first, then to a pronoun, verb, and noun.

In the second step, the semantic representation provides meaning to the words, setting the agent of the sentence as "I" and the object as "Linda." From this interpretation alone, however, we don't know who the pronoun "I" stands for.

In the last step, the semantic interpretation is expanded further based on the context (obtained from information that precedes or follows this sentence) or the world knowledge, thus completing the semantic interpretation. For example, the agent might be John and the instrument used for examination the stethoscope.

When you ask a question, the system will put together an intelligent response using its semantic knowledge. If we ask, "Who examined Linda," an unintelligent response would be "I." Since the fact "I examined Linda" was represented in expanded semantic form as described above, the system can intelligently respond with the answer "John."

Besides the above, there are many other NLU methods. Statistical models such as Hidden Markov Models (Jelinek, 1998) work by constructing the probability of the occurrence of a word given the surrounding words. Bayesian networks (Kim, Hong, & Cho, 2007; Blei, Ng, & Jordan, 2003) and neural networks (Bengio, Ducharme, Vincent, & Jauvin, 2003; Collobert & Weston, 2008) have also been successfully used for NLU. Other interesting research in the field includes artificial humor (Wen, Baym, Tamuz, Teevan, Dumais, & Kalai, 2015; Mihalcea & Strapparava, 2006) and neural machine translation (Bahdanau, Cho, & Bengio, 2015).

Even when a computer is able to understand or have conversations in natural language, that doesn't automatically mean it can match human intelligence. How do we test to see if the computer can understand and intelligently respond like a human? We'll examine this question in the next chapter.

9. IDENTIFYING INTELLIGENCE

Objectives

- ☐ Introduce the Turing Test for intelligence
- ☐ Explain the concept of partial intelligence and general intelligence
- ☐ Understand the concept of super intelligence and its potential dangers
- ☐ Understand the current state of AI, including the Loebner prize

The **Turing test** is the classical test for artificial intelligence, first proposed in the 1950s (Turing, 1950). In the test, a human interrogator interacts with both a human and a computer through a text interface. Based on her conversations, the human tries to guess which conversation partner is the computer (see Figure 9-1). According to the Turing test, the computer is considered intelligent if the human cannot reliably distinguish which conversation partner is the computer.

Figure 9-1: In the Turing test, the interrogator is trying to guess which conversation partner is the human, and which is the computer.

The Turing test is not perfect (Hayes & Ford, 1995; Cohen, 2005). For example, a computer may trick a novice interrogator by simulating common typographical errors. It is also worth noting that the test is only for human behavior. If a computer passes the Turing test, it may not be good for scheduling surgeries. For instance, we obviously cannot expect a dance teacher to schedule surgeries without any training, even though she is intelligent. In real life, a responsible dance teacher might say, "I am sorry, I don't know how to schedule surgeries. I am a dance teacher. Ask the nurse." Or a malicious dance teacher may pretend to be a surgery scheduler. Thus, what it means to have 'true' intelligence is an open question, as is whether the Turing test actually evaluates for true intelligence.

The Turing test test does not evaluate **partial intelligence** where the expectation is human-level performance in a narrow area. Some notable applications of partial intelligence include a natural language translation program, a program that displays an advertisement a user might be interested in, a program that decides when to trade a stock based on information it receives from the market, a diagnostic program used in medicine, and a program that raises an alarm by monitoring patient vitals in an Intensive Care Unit (ICU).

To see if a system performs at human level in a narrow domain, experts might evaluate it. For example, a team of doctors can test that an expert system comes up with the correct diagnosis given the symptoms, much like they evaluate a medical student to see if she is qualified. For an expert system to make a correct diagnosis, it doesn't have to understand natural language.

The modern definitions of AI accommodate partial intelligence. Here is one definition: AI may be defined as *the ability to perceive, think and act independently* (Winston, 1992). For example, a computer can perceive the emergency nature of an incoming case, think about what must be done, and act by scheduling the emergency procedures and alerting the required personnel. A computer can perceive an equipment failure while a surgery is in progress and make new equipment available with rescheduling.

The traditional AI approach of trying to create adult intelligence (called General Intelligence, or GI) has been largely unsuccessful for two central reasons. First, the human brain is very complex, and we do not understand all of its features sufficiently to mimic it with a generalized AI system. Second, AI researchers have been focusing on solving various problems considered simpler than GI (such as partial intelligence), and their work is scattered all across the board. GI would need us to integrate all partial intelligence research areas in a meaningful way.

Some researchers think that while achieving GI is difficult, once a machine can reach the intelligence level of an infant, it can then learn on its own (Nilsson N. J., 2005; Turing, 1950). For example, an "infant machine" can be gifted to children to pet. The machine learns how to do simple puzzles or sing nursery rhymes by observing children. Like children, the machine learns by forming general patterns from specific examples and develops into a "child machine." We could then send the "child machine" through school, college, and some specific medical training program. The machine may then be able to work as a scheduling nurse in the ORoom. If you are interested, Nilsson (2005) discusses the core capabilities a "child machine" would need to possess in order to learn on its own by interacting with its environment.

9.1. Super Intelligence

If machines can achieve GI, they will have some advantages over us. They are reliable, they are fast, and they can work round the clock without fatigue. They can communicate with other machines at lightning speed and gather information from massive databases and the Internet. Most importantly, an intelligent machine can try to improve itself (e.g., by performing AI research). If that happens, we will find ourselves in unchartered territory (Bostrom, 2014)!

Machines could get smarter at a much faster rate than we can ever imagine, causing what is called an intelligence explosion (Kurzweil, 2005). A few researchers draw parallels between an intelligence explosion and nuclear chain reaction. An uncontrolled intelligence explosion could cause a technological singularity that is unpredictable or unimaginable with human-level intelligence.

In this chapter, we talked about Turing test and its limitations as an effective test for AI. The Loebner prize competition is considered the first instantiation of Turing test (Loebner, 1991), which has been conducted every year since its inception in 1991. Of the three award levels, Gold and Silver had never awarded at the time of this writing. There have been many Bronze winners.

While General Intelligence (GI) still remains as a challenge, researchers have started speculating about super intelligence and potential ramifications of it. The next chapter concludes this book with some speculations on the future trajectory of AI.

10. CONCLUSIONS AND WHERE TO GO FROM HERE

Objectives

- ☐ Summarize AI topics covered in this book
- ☐ Learn how AI relates to other disciplines
- ☐ Explore the future of AI, its potential and its pitfalls
- ☐ Understand what ethical AI is all about

In this book, we saw various methods that help computers intelligently solve problems. First, we saw how AI can solve the ORoom scheduling problem. Heuristic search methods focus on promising paths, thereby possibly reaching the goal much more quickly. Genetic algorithms evolve solutions by imitating the natural evolution process. Genetic programming helps us to automatically generate computer programs to solve real life problems.

Second, we looked at how expert systems can diagnose diseases by encoding domain knowledge as rules. They can work forward from a set of observable facts and deduct conclusions or perform actions, or they can backtrack from specified goals and prove or disprove them by exploring the facts. Fuzzy expert systems go a step further by supporting real-life rules. We also saw how neural networks acquire domain knowledge and adapt to the situations by self learning, whether supervised or unsupervised. We also saw how game trees help hospital administration to weigh facts and determine the winning strategy against competition.

10.1. AI and Other Disciplines

Although AI is firmly rooted in computer science, it has a solid relationship with other disciplines as well. For example, some experts believe that philosophy has to make big strides before AI can have any major breakthroughs, because we need to significantly enhance our own understanding about human cognition, the mind and consciousness.

AI works with psychology to create humanoid robots and robots that can express emotions. Psychology helps AI to understand how people think and interact.

Neurophysiology helps AI study brain structures and design new neural networks to simulate intelligence. Genetic algorithms have foundations in biology and, in particular, genetics (Mendel, 1866) and Darwin's theory of evolution (Darwin, 1859) by natural selection.

For the most part, natural language, being an expression of human intelligence, does not strictly follow any known set of rules or representations. Research in computational linguistics tries to develop models (e.g., rule-based or statistical) for natural language. AI taps into these linguistic models for understanding and generating natural language.

AI is even connected with law. For example, suppose a city has an ordinance banning vehicles idling in front of schools in an attempt to improve the air quality. Will a refrigerated truck stopped for delivery be in violation of this ordinance? What about emergency vehicles? Is there any other law define specific exceptions? Is there any precedent? The deliberation process has striking similarities to inference procedures in knowledge based systems.

Today, AI has been seamlessly integrated with many mainstream engineering systems to the degree that they are not even popularly recognized as AI any more. Electronic stability control or anti-lock brake systems are good examples.

10.2. The Future of Artificial Intelligence

The classical expectation of AI is that computers should be able to fully interact with us in natural language, just as a human would. Clearly, we aren't there yet, or else we'd be able to buy a generally intelligent helper robot for our homes, for example.

The partial intelligence approach of AI has improved applications such as search engines, financial fraud detection, medical diagnosis, customer relations management, transportation, augmented reality and gaming. In the future, AI will be used to analyze and discover correlations in an ever increasing number of data streams. AI has been instrumental in creating military robots, industrial robots and humanoid robots. The availability of great processing power and huge memory capacities has been instrumental in making great strides in all these areas. This trend is likely to continue as exponential growth continues in processing power, memory space availability, and communication speed.

While the partial intelligence approach has been very successful in solving many real-life problems, the toughest problem of all still remains: replicating human intelligence. Given that most predictions on AI have been largely inaccurate, we don't exactly know when that goal will be achieved.

Whole brain emulation is one approach to producing GI. The idea is to scan a human brain in detail and use image processing to document neurons and their interconnections (Markram, February 2006). Once a brain is fully mapped, we can artificially create neurons and interconnections, hopefully creating GI. The blue brain project has been trying to do exactly that. Studies have also tried to recognize and reproduce different (Grossberg, 1988) structure and regions of the brain. However, it is unclear whether a simplistic emulation of neurons can capture GI.

Apart from whole brain simulation, there are many approaches for creating GI (Beal & Winston, 2009; Dyson, 1997). The Cyc project, started in 1980s, attempts to encode common sense knowledge using first order predicate logic. Soar (Laird, Newell, & Rosenbloom, 1987) is an interesting cognitive architecture that can be used to develop intelligent systems.

The evolution of human beings as the most intelligent creature on earth has been very slow (Cummins & Allen, 1998). It happened over millions of years, and helped us survive in our environment. Computers are good at solving problems that are very difficult for us, but fail terribly at problems that we find easy. Perhaps these problems are not simple per se; it's just that we have developed the complex capability to easily solve these problems over generations because we needed to in order to survive (Drozdek, 1995). For example, it is natural for us to recognize a bear when we see one, but it is difficult to program a computer to do the same thing reliably. On the other hand, our brain is not the best at dealing with mathematical calculations. Quickly computing the sixteenth power of ten is not something we have ever needed for survival, but it's something easily done by a computer.

Of course, computational speed is only one aspect of problem solving. The other aspect is coming up with methods and structures to solve difficult problems. It turns out that we have not yet understood these basic building blocks of intelligent behavior (Skinner, 1953). Once we do, it may turn out that we don't need much processing speed after all.

If we are able to achieve GI, however it's done, what comes next? How are we going to use it? Are we going to replace human beings with AI systems? Perhaps human jobs will one day be replaced by easily replicable AI machines.

Will AI be ethical? If forced to make a choice, how does a self-driving car choose between the only two choices available: steer away to save the driver from a truck coming head-on at high speed, or potentially harm the five children playing on the sidewalk? Will an AI digital assistant manipulate customers into buying unneeded products to increase profit? Will a military robot use overwhelming force to maximize kills, risking collateral damage?

Will AI be used for the good of mankind? Robots are already used in dangerous professions to replace humans (Kumar, et al., 2008). Unfortunately, robots can just as easily be used to harm others.

In a 1942 short story titled *Runaround* (Asimov, 1942), Isaac Asimov introduces three famous laws of robotics. In essence, they are: 1) a robot may not injure a human being by action or inaction; 2) a robot must obey all orders given to it by human beings so long as it is not in violation of the first law; 3) a robot must protect its own existence as long as it doesn't violate the first and the second laws. Maybe, as a community, we should develop similar ethical laws for the AIs we build.

If GI ultimately leads to super intelligence (SI) and singularity, how do we make sure that machines would have our best interest on their mind? What is the guarantee that SI won't override the ethical laws? Can SI be an existential threat?

Many questions still remain. Could we upload ourselves to machines and get rid of all the physical limitations of our body? Can we achieve immortality by getting rid of our biological body? Or keep our biological body and augment it with technology? Despite the exciting possibilities that will continue to open up, AI is a very humbling field where we have more questions than answers.

In this book, we have seen some powerful methods for achieving partial artificial intelligence. These methods coupled with exponential advances in technology may put us on a path to general intelligence or even super intelligence. We hope that you will continue to explore the ideas we have presented and find ways to use them to solve problems you care deeply about.

APPENDIX A: SEARCH METHODS

This appendix is for the advanced reader with some knowledge of data structures such as graph, tree, list and stack. Some programming background will also be helpful. The pseudo code is pretty close to C++ or Java, if you plan on implementing the search methods.

A.1. Depth First Search (DFS)

```
//For a Graph g and the search starting point start_node
dfs(Graph g, Node start_node, Node goal_node)
{
 Stack s = {};  //initialize the stack s as empty

 visited_list = {};  //Initialize the list of visited nodes as empty
 s.push(start_node); //push the starting node into the top of
                     //the stack

 while (s is not empty)
   {
   u = s.pop();  //pop the top element of the stack s
   if (u not in visited_list) //if the node has not been visited before
       {
       if u is the goal_node
             return success;
       add u to the visited_list
       for each w that is the unvisited neighbor of u
               s.push(w);  //push all unvisited neighbors of u into stack
       } //end if
   }    //end while
  return failure;
} //end dfs
```

A.2. Breadth First Search (BFS)

```
//For a Graph g and the search starting point start_node
bfs(Graph g, Node start_node, Node goal_node)
{
 List l = {};   //initialize the list s as empty

 visited_list = {}; //Initialize the list of visited nodes as empty
 l.push(start_node); //add starting node into the end of the list

 while (s is not empty)
   {
   u = l.pop();  //pop the first element of the List
   if (u not in visited_list) //if the node has not been visited before
      {
       if u is the goal_node
           return success;
       add u to the visited_list
       for each w that is the unvisited neighbor of u
            l.append(w);  //put all unvisited neighbors of u into list
      } //end if
   }    //end while
   return failure;
} //end bfs
```

Note that BFS is the same us DFS except that the data structure we use for BFS is a list (FIFO) than a stack (LIFO).

A.3. Simple Hill Climbing

```
//For a Graph g and the search starting point start_node
SimpleHillClimbing(Graph g, Node start_node, Node goal_node)
{
Stack s = {};   //initialize the stack s as empty
visited_list = {}; //Initialize the list of visited nodes as empty
s.push(start_node); //push the starting node into the top of
                    //the stack
while (s is not empty)
  {
  u = s.pop();  //pop the top element of the stack s
  if (u not in visited_list) //if the node has not been visited before
     {
      if u is the goal_node
          return success;
       add u to the visited_list
       for each w that is the unvisited neighbor of u
           { // check if w is promising
           if (w.h() >= u.h()) // h() is the heuristic method
               {
               s.push(w);//add a promising neighbor of u to stack
               break; //  break here for non restarting hill climbing
               }
           }
     } //end if
  }   //end while
  return failure;
} //end SimpleHillClimbing
```

Simple Hill Climbing is very similar to DFS except that only the promising neighbor is explored. Difference is highlighted.

Note that in many cases it is not very straight forward to know that the node u is the goal. So depending on application, modification may be needed to determine that the search reached the goal node.

Without the break statement in the above code, hill climbing will backtrack and continue exploring promising path after reaching a node with no outlet (e.g., leaf node).

A.4. Steepest Ascent Hill Climbing

```
//For a Graph g and the search starting point start_node
SteepestAscentHillClimbing(Graph g, Node start_node, Node goal_node)
{
 Stack s = {};  //initialize the stack s as empty

visited_list = {}; //Initialize the list of visited nodes as empty

 s.push(start_node); //push the starting node into the top of
                     //the stack
 while (s is not empty)
   {
   u = s.pop();  //pop the top element of the stack s
   if (u not in visited_list) //if the node has not been visited before
      {
      if u is the goal_node
          return success;
      add u to the visited_list
      w=u.get_most _promising_neighbor();
      if (w is not null && w.h() > u.h())
          s.push(w); //Push the most promising neighbor
                     // into the stack if that is better than current node
      else
          break;  // break here for non restarting hill climbing
      } //end if
   }   //end while
   return failure;
} // SteepestAscentHillClimbing
```

Steepest Ascent Hill Climbing is very similar to DFS/Simple Hill Climbing except that only the most promising neighbor (based on heuristic value) is explored. Difference is highlighted. How can you modify the code to make the steepest ascent hill climbing restart?

A.5. Best First Search

```
//For a Graph g and the search starting point start_node
// pl is a PriorityList on the increasing heuristic value of each node

bestfs(Graph g, Node start_node, Node goal_node)
{
 PriorityList pl = {};   //initialize the priority list pl as empty

 visited_list = {}; //Initialize the list of visited nodes as empty
 pl.push(start_node); //add starting node to the list
 while (s is not empty)
  {
  u = pl.pop();  //pop the first element of the List
  if (u not in visited_list) //if the node has not been visited before
     {
     if u is the goal_node
          return success;
     add u to the visited_list
     for each w that is the unvisited neighbor of u
             pl.push(w);  //put all unvisited neighbors of u into list
     } //end if
  }    //end while
  return failure;
} //end bestfs
```

Note that Best First Search is the same as Breadth First Search (BFS) except that the list is a priority list based on the heuristic value of nodes. Difference is highlighted.

A.6. A*

A* uses two lists: *ol* to open nodes and *cl* to store nodes those are finished exploring. We also need to keep track of more information within the node:

```
Node{
  ad; //actual distance
  ed; //estimated remaining distance
  h;   // heuristic value, h=ad+ed
  Node *p; //pointer to the predecessor.
}
```

ad is the actual distance to the node from start node
ed is the estimated remaining distance from the node

h is actually the sum of ad and ed, but for efficiency reasons we store h.

The variable p is the pointer to the predecessor to keep track of the path from the source_node to the node. The pointer, p, will be updated if we find a better path to reach the node based on dynamic programming principle.

```
//astar algorithm on graph g from start node to the goal node
// open_list is a PriorityList on increasing order of h
astar(Graph g, Node start_node, Node goal_node)
{
PriorityList open_list=start_node;
 closed_list={}; //Set closed list as empty
while open_list is not empty
{
  pop the first node from open_list; say that node is r;
  for each successor s of r
     {
     if s is the goal_node
           return s;      // s.p points to the best path
     if s is in the closed_list
           continue; // closed - continue from start of the for loop
     ed = hfx(); // use the heuristic function to find the estimated
                   //distance from s to the goal node
     ad = r.ad + distance between s and r; // find the actual distance
     h = ad + ed; // calculate the heuristic value
     if s is already in the open_list
        {
        if s.h < h
           continue; // existing path is better
        else
           pop s from the open_list; //existing path is bad so remove it
        }
     s.p  = r;    // indicate r as their parent
     s.ad = ad;  s.ed = ed; //set actual and estimated distances
     s.h = h;      //initialize the heuristic value
     add s to open_list;
     } //end for
     add r to the closed_list;  //Finished examining all successors of r
  } //end while
  return failure;  //Search failed to find the goal node
} //end astar
```

APPENDIX B: NEURAL NETWORK LEARNING MORE COMPLEX LOGIC

In this appendix you will understand the limitations of a single neuron. You will learn how to set up a network to learn the XOR logic.

Say, the nurse is trying to schedule a c-section. She has a pool of two trusted neonatologists. So she calls them to see one of them would be available. The ideal situation is one of them can attend. She won't be able to schedule the c-section, if none is available or it would be expensive if both neonatologists arrive. This type of logic is called Exclusive OR (XOR). Figure B-1 shows input/output characteristics for XOR.

(Input 1)	(Input 2)	(Desired Output)
0	0	0
0	1	1
1	0	1
1	1	0

Figure B-1: A description of the inputs for XOR, and the desired output in those cases.

Can a 2-input neuron learn the XOR logic?

(See the next page.)

Assuming that both input weights are set as 0.5, we get the following outputs for various input combinations as shown in Figure B-2:

Input 1	Input 2	Input 1 x Weight 1	Input 2 x Weight 2	Total	Actual Output
0	0	0	0	0	0 ☑
0	1	0	0.5	0.5	1 ☑
1	0	0.5	0	0.5	1 ☑
1	1	0.5	0.5	1.0	1 ☒

Figure B-2: Summary of tests applied to a neuron with a threshold of 0.5 and weights of 0.5.

We know that neuron failed the test when the both inputs are 1. See if you can make the neuron to learn XOR logic. After trying numerous weight combinations, you will eventually realize that it is impossible for the neuron to learn the XOR logic. Why?

A single neuron can only learn linearly separable functions. In other words, you should be able to separate output 1's and 0's by drawing a line.

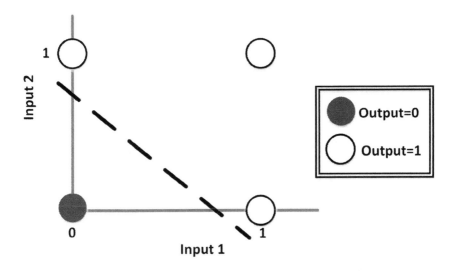

Figure B-3: Linear separation of output values

Figure B-3 visually represents the Input/Output characteristics shown in Figure B-4:

(Input 1)	(Input 2)	(Desired Output)
0	0	0
0	1	1
1	0	1
1	1	1

Figure B-4: Linearly Separable Input/Output characteristics.

The x-axis shows Input 1 and the y-axis shows Input 2. Shaded circles indicate an output of 0 and clear circles indicate an output of 1. We can draw a line to separate the groups of 0s and 1s. So a single neuron can learn this logic. In fact this is the same example we saw in Chapter 5.

What about XOR? Figure B-5 shows Input/Output combinations for XOR:

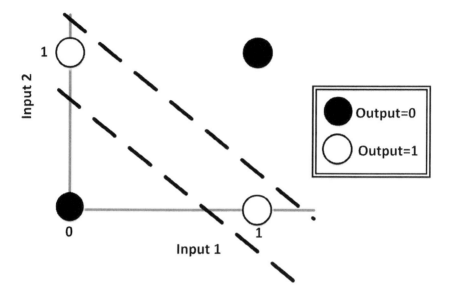

Figure B-5:XOR Inputs/Output combination

We know from Figure B-5 that 0s and 1s cannot be separated by drawing a single line. In fact two lines are needed for doing so. So to learn XOR logic, we need more than one neurons.

Say, we have three neurons. The first neuron can learn to fire if inputs are above the bottom dashed line. The second neuron can learn to fire if the inputs are below the top dashed line. A third neuron can learn to fire if (and only if) both neurons fire. So a three neuron network can learn XOR logic.

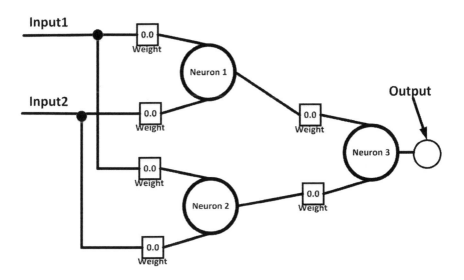

Figure B-6: An ANN capable of learning XOR logic

Figure B-6 shows the three neuron network. Try training the XOR logic by adjusting the weights.

APPENDIX C: FUZZY EXPERT SYSTEM

This appendix shows how a simple fuzzy expert system can be constructed for stroke risk assessment and how to perform fuzzy inference.

Say, we have a simple expert system for assessing a person's stroke risk. The expert system has two rules.

The first rule:
R1: if age is Old
         risk = High

You may have noticed that our rules state "risk = High" rather than "risk = true." This is because, in reality, the risk is not as crisp as true and false. We define the fuzzy set High in Figure C-1.

The degree of truth increases as age goes up from 50 to 75, as shown in Figure C-1. Someone who is 50 is old with a degree of truth 0 – in other words, they are considered young. Someone who is 75 is old with a degree of truth 1.0. A 70 year old is also old, but with lesser degree of truth: 0.8. We assume that the maximum age is 125 years.

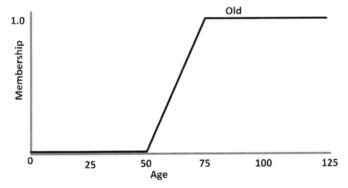

Figure C-1: Fuzzy set for age.

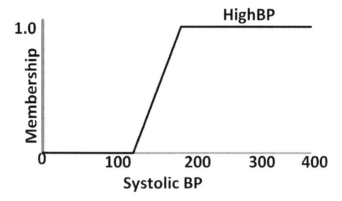

Figure C-2: Fuzzy set for systolic pressure.

Now consider an additional rule based on high blood pressure for the expert system:

R2: if systolic blood pressure is HighBP
        risk = High

Figure C-2   shows the membership function for Systolic BP. According to the figure, the risk steadily increases as blood pressure (BP) rises from 120 mmHg to 180 mmHg.   We assume that the maximum BP is 400 mmHg.

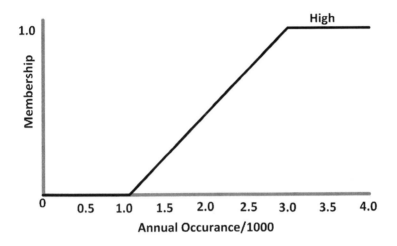

Figure C-3: Stroke Occurrence Risk -- one incidence or less per 1000 is considered low risk whereas 3 incidences or more per 1000 is considered high risk

According to Figure C-3, an annual occurrence of 1 stroke or less per 1000 people is considered low risk. Three or more occurrences is considered high risk. For occurrences between 1.0 and 3.0, the membership values vary. We assume that the maximum stroke risk is 4 annual occurrences per 1000 people.

Fuzzyfication

Say we want to find out the stroke risk for a 70 year old man with a systolic BP of 140 using our fuzzy expert system.

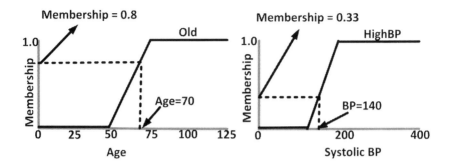

Figure C-4: Fuzzification of inputs.

Since a fuzzy expert system has its rules defined in terms of fuzzy values, the first step is to convert the inputs to fuzzy values; this is called **fuzzification**.

In other words, we have to find the membership values of inputs in the applicable fuzzy sets. From Figure C-4, we see that the age 70 is *Old* with a membership value (degree of truth) of 0.8. Likewise, the membership value for BP 140 in *HighBP* is 0.33.

So after fuzzification, the input values are:

age = *Old* (membership value = 0.8)

systolic BP = *HighBP* (membership value = 0.33)

Fuzzy Inference

Once we have fuzzified the inputs, the rules then work concurrently on fuzzified inputs to generate multiple results as described below.

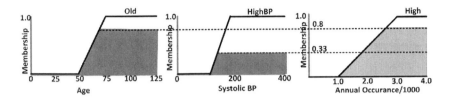

Figure C-5: Fuzzy inference.

Let us look at the first rule:

R1: if age is Old
        risk = High

The rule says that if someone is Old, then the risk is High. Based on our input, we are not certain that the person is Old. The degree of truth is 0.8, so the rule infers that the degree of truth of the risk being High is also 0.8 (see Figure C-5).

Now consider the second rule:

R2: if systolic blood pressure is HighBP
        risk = High

Fuzzification of systolic BP gives us a membership value 0.33 in HighBP. Therefore, the rule R2 infers that the risk is High with a degree of truth 0.33.

In fuzzy expert systems, usually all rules contribute to the final result. Rules R1 and R2 provide two different membership values for risk (0.8 and 0.33 respectively). In this case, the inference engine will consider the maximum of the two values as the membership value for risk (0.8).

Defuzzification

From the inference described earlier, we saw that the degree of truth for the risk being High is 0.8. However, we may like a crisp value for risk in terms of number of annual stroke occurrences. The process of finding the crisp value is called **defuzzification**.

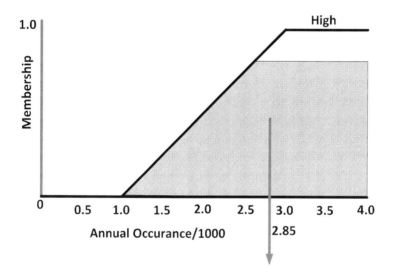

Figure C-6: Defuzzified output.

The shaded area in Figure C-6 shows the fuzzy set High clipped at membership (0.8). How do we defuzzify the risk? One method is to find the center of gravity (centroid) of the shaded area. The centroid is shown with a downward arrow as above.

The centroid an x-coordinate of 2.85. So, according to the expert system, the stroke risk is 2.85 annual occurrences per 1000 people for a 70 year old man with a systolic BP of 140.

In the previous examples, we used only one fuzzy set for each variable. We can in fact use more than one fuzzy sets. For example, we may use three fuzzy sets (Low, Medium and High) to define risk.

Imagine that we have three rules: Rule A says the risk is Low; Rule B says the risk is Medium; and Rule C says the risk is High. Say, the shaded areas in   Figure C-7 represent the membership values determined by these rules.

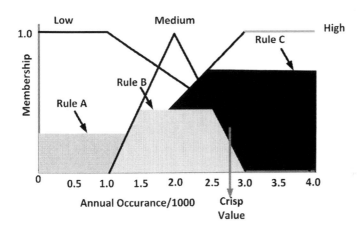

Figure C-7: General Defuzzification

Just like before, we can determine the crisp value of risk by determining the centroid of the combined shaded area (Negnevitsky, 2004).

11. BIBLIOGRAPHY

Adelson-Velsky, G. M., Arlazarov, V. L., Bitman, A. R., Zhivotovsky, A. A., & Uskov, A. V. (1970). Programming a computer to play chess. *Russian Mathematical Surveys* , *25*, 221-262.

Aho, A. V., Hopcroft, J. E., & Ullman, J. D. (1974). *The design and analysis of computer algorithms.* Addison-Wesley.

Aikins, J. S., Kunz, J. C., Shortliffe, E. H., & Fallat, R. J. (1983). PUFF: An expert system for interpretation of pulmonary function data. *Computers in Biomedical Research* , 199-208.

Alander, J. T. (1994). *An indexed bibliography of genetic algorithms: years 1957--1993.* Vaasa, Finland: Art of CAD ltd.

Allen, J. (1995). *Natural Language Understanding (2Nd Ed.).* Redwood City, CA, USA: Benjamin-Cummings.

Anderson, M., & Anderson, S. L. (2007). Machine ethics: Creating an ethical intelligent agent. *AI Magazine* .

Anthony, M., & Bartlett, P. L. (2009). *Neural network learning: Theoretical foundations* (1 ed.). New York, NY, USA: Cambridge University Press.

Araujo, L. (2004). Genetic programming for natural language parsing. In M. Keijzer, U.-M. O'Reilly, S. M. Lucas, E. Costa, & T. Soule (Ed.), *Genetic Programming 7th European Conf., EuroGP 2004. 3003*, pp. 230-239. Springer-Verlag.

Ashby, W. R. (1954). *Design for a brain.* Wiley.

Asimov, I. (1942 йил March). Runaround. *Astounding Science Fiction* . Street & Smith.

Bäck, T. (1996). *Evolutionary algorithms in theory and practice: evolution strategies, evolutionary programming, genetic algorithms.* Oxford, UK: Oxford University Press.

Bahdanau, D., Cho, K., & Bengio, Y. (2015). Neural machine translation by jointly learning to align and translate. *ICLR.*

Banko, M., Brill, E., Dumais, S., & Lin, J. (2002). AskMSR: Question answering using the Worldwide Web. *Proc. of 2002 AAAI Spring Symposium on Mining Answers from Texts and Knowledge Bases,* (pp. 7-9).

Banzhaf, W., Francone, F. D., Keller, R. E., & Nordin, P. (1998). *Genetic Programming: An introduction: on the automatic evolution of computer programs and Its applications.* San Francisco, CA, USA: Morgan Kaufmann Publishers Inc.

Baum, E. B., & Haussler, D. (1989). What size net gives valid generalization? *Neural Computing , 1* (1), 151-160.

Baum, E. B., Boneh, D., & Garrett, C. (1995). On genetic algorithms. *Proc. of the Eighth Annual Conf. on Computational Learning Theory* (pp. 230-239). New York, NY, USA: ACM.

Beal, D. F. (1980). An analysis of minimax. In M. R. Clarke (Ed.), *Advances in Computer Chess 2* (pp. 103-109). Edinburgh.

Beal, J., & Winston, P. H. (2009). Guest editors' introduction: the new frontier of human-level Artificial Intelligence. *IEEE Intelligent Systems , 24* (4), 21-23.

Bellman, R. E. (1978). *An introduction to Artificial Intelligence: Can computers think?* Boyd.

Bengio, Y., Ducharme, R., Vincent, P., & Jauvin, C. (2003). A neural probabilistic language model. *Jl. of Machine Learning Research ,* 1137–1155.

Bishop, C. M. (1995). *Neural networks for pattern recognition.* New York, NY, USA: Oxford University Press.

Blazewicz, J., Lenstra, J., & Kan, A. (1981). *Scheduling subject to resource constraints: classification and complexity.* Elsevier .

Blei, D. M., Ng, A. Y., & Jordan, M. I. (2003). Latent dirichlet allocation. *Jl. of Machine Learning Research* , 993-1022.

Boden, M. A. (1990). *The philosophy of artificial intelligence.* Oxford, New York: Oxford University Press.

Bostrom, N. (2014). *Superintelligence: Paths, Dangers, Strategies* (1 ed.). Oxford, UK: Oxford University Press.

Brown, E. W. (2012). Watson: The Jeopardy! challenge and beyond. *Proc. of the 35th Intl. ACM SIGIR Conf. on Research and Development in Information Retrieval* (pp. 1020-1020). ACM.

Bruner, J. S., Goodnow, J. J., & Austin, G. A. (1956). *A study of thinking.* New York: John Wiley.

Buchanan, B. G. (2005). A (very) brief history of Artificial Intelligence. *AI Magazine* , *26* (4), 53-60.

Buchanan, B. G., & Shortliffe, E. H. (1984). *Rule Based Expert Systems: The Mycin Experiments of the Stanford Heuristic Programming Project (The Addison-Wesley Series in Artificial Intelligence).* Reading, MA, USA: Addison-Wesley.

Buehler, M., Iagnemma, K., & Singh, S. (2007). *The 2005 DARPA Grand Challenge: The Great Robot Race* (1 ed.). Springer Publishing Company, Incorporated.

Campbell, M., Hoane, J. A., & Hsu, F.-h. (2002). Deep Blue. *Artificial Intelligence* , *134* (1-2), 57-83.

Cardoen, B., Demeulemeester, E., & Beliën, J. (2010). Operating room planning and scheduling: A literature review. *European Jl. of Operational Research*, *201* (3), 921-932.

Charniak, E. (1987). *Artificial intelligence programming*. Erlbaum Associates.

Charniak, E., & McDermott, D. (1985). *Introduction to Artificial Intelligence*. Boston, MA, USA: Addison-Wesley.

Cheeseman, P. (1988). An inquiry into computer understanding. *Computational Intelligence*, *4*, 58-66.

Cheeseman, P., Kanefsky, B., & Taylor, W. M. (1991). Where the really hard problems are. *IJCAI* (pp. 331-337). Morgan Kaufmann.

Church, K. W. (2003). Speech and language processing: where have we been and where are we going? *Interspeech*. ISCA.

Cohen, P. (2005). If not the Turing Test, then what. *AI Magazine*.

Collobert, R., & Weston, J. (2008). A unified architecture for natural language processing: deep neural networks with multitask learning. *Proc. of the 25th Intl. Conf. on machine learning*.

Copeland, J. (1993). *Artificial Intelligence: A philosophical introduction*. Blackwell.

Cormen, T. H., Leiserson, C. E., Rivest, R. L., & Stein, C. (2009). *Introduction to Algorithms, Third Edition* (3 ed.). The MIT Press.

Cowan, J. D., & Sharp, D. H. (1988). Neural nets and artificial intelligence. *Daedalus*, *117*, 85-121.

Croft, B., Metzler, D., & Strohman, T. (2009). *Search Engines: Information Retrieval in Practice* (1 ed.). USA: Addison-Wesley Publishing Company.

Cummins, D. D., & Allen, C. (1998). *The evolution of mind.* Oxford, UK: Oxford University Press.

Darwin, C. R. (1859). *The origin of species.* London: John Murray.

Davis, E. (1990). *Representations of Commonsense Knowledge.* Morgan Kaufman.

Davis, L. (1985). Job shop scheduling with genetic algorithms. *Proc. of the 1st Intl. Conf. on Genetic Algorithms* (pp. 136-140). Hillsdale, NJ, USA: Erlbaum Associates.

Dean, T. L., & Wellman, M. P. (1991). *Planning and Control.* San Francisco, CA: Morgan Kaufman.

Dechter, R., & Pearl, J. (1985). Generalized best-first search strategies and the optimality of A*. *JACM , 32* (3), 505-536.

Dennett, D. C. (1978). Why you can't make a computer that feels pain. *Synthese , 38* (3).

Dreyfus, H. L. (1972). *What computers can't do: A critique of artificial reason* (1 ed.). Harper.

Dreyfus, H. L. (1979). *What computers can't do: The limits of Artificial Intelligence* (Revised ed.). Harper.

Dreyfus, H. L. (1992). *What computers still can't do: A critique of artificial reason.* MIT Press.

Dreyfus, S. E. (1969). An appraisal of some shortest-paths algorithms. *Operations Research , 17*, 395-412.

Drozdek, A. (1998). Human Intelligence and Turing Test. *AI and Society , 12* (4), 315-321.

Drozdek, A. (1995). What if computers could think? *AI and Society , 9* (4), 389-395.

Dyer, M. (1983). *In-depth understanding.* MIT Press.

Dyson, G. B. (1997). *Darwin among the machines: The evolution of global intelligence.* Boston, MA, USA: Addison-Wesley Longman Publishing Co., Inc.

Erman, L. D., Hayes-Roth, F., Lesser, V. R., & Reddy, D. R. (1980). The Hearsay-II speech-understanding system: {I}ntegrating knowledge to resolve uncertainty. *Computing Surveys , 12* (2), 213-253.

Etzioni, O., Hanks, S., Weld, D., Draper, D., Lesh, N., & Williamson, M. (1992). An approach to planning with incomplete information. *Proc. of the 3rd Intl. Conf. on Principles of Knowledge Representation and Reasoning.*

Ferrucci, D. A. (2012). Introduction to "This is Watson". *IBM J. Res. Dev. , 56* (3), 235-249.

Fogel, L., Owens, A., & Walsh, M. (1966). *Artificial intelligence through simulated evolution.* Chichester, WS, UK: Wiley.

Forbus, K. D., & Kleer, J. D. (1993). *Building problem Solvers.* Cambridge, MA, USA: MIT Press.

Goldberg, D. E. (1989). *Genetic algorithms in search, optimization and machine learning.* Addison-Wesley.

Gomes, C. P. (2000). Artificial Intelligence and Operations Research: Challenges and opportunities in planning and scheduling. *Knowl. Eng. Rev. , 15* (1), 1-10.

Gorry, G. A. (1973). Computer-assisted clinical decision-making. *Methods of Information in Medicine , 12* (1), 45-51.

Grossberg, S. (1988). *The adaptive brain I.* Elsevier Science Ltd.

Grosz, B. J., Sparck Jones, K., & Webber, B. L. (Eds.). (1986). *Readings in Natural Language Processing.* Morgan Kaufman.

Guizzo, E. (2011, October). How Google's self-driving car works. *How Google's self-driving car works* . (E. Guizzo, Ed.) New York, NY: IEEE.

Guzzoni, D., Baur, C., & Cheyer, A. (n.d.). Active : A unified platform for building intelligent web interaction assistants.

Haugeland, J. (1985). *Artificial Intelligence: The very idea.* Cambridge, MA, USA: Massachusetts Institute of Technology.

Hayes, P. J. (1977). On semantic nets, frames and associations. *IJCAI 77*, (pp. 99-107).

Hayes, P., & Ford, K. (1995). Turing test considered harmful. *Proc. of the 14th Intl. Joint Conf. on Artificial Intelligence - Volume 1* (pp. 972-977). San Francisco, CA, USA: Morgan Kaufmann Publishers Inc.

Haykin, S. (1998). *Neural networks: A comprehensive foundation* (2nd ed.). Upper Saddle River, NJ, USA: Prentice Hall PTR.

Hertz, J., Krogh, A., & Palmer, R. G. (1991). *Introduction to the theory of neural computation.* Addison-Wesley.

Hsu, F.-H. (2002). *Behind Deep Blue: Building the computer that defeated the world chess champion.* Princeton, NJ, USA: Princeton University Press.

Huang, X., Acero, A., & Hon, H.-W. (2001). *Spoken language processing: A guide to theory, algorithm, and system development* (1 ed.). Upper Saddle River, NJ, USA: Prentice Hall.

Hubel, D. H. (1995). *Eye, brain, and vision (Scientific American library, No 22)* (2 ed.). W. H. Freeman.

Humphrys, M. (1995). How my program passed the Turing test. In *Parsing the Turing test* (pp. 237-260). Springer Science.

Huyn, N., Dechter, R., & Pearl, J. (1980). Probabilistic analysis of the complexity of A*. *Artificial Intelligence* , *15* (3), 241-254.

Jackson, P. (1998). *Introduction to Expert Systems* (3rd ed.). Boston, MA, USA: Addison-Wesley.

Jain, S. (1999). *Systems that learn : an introduction to learning theory.* MIT Press.

Jelinek, F. (1998). *Statistical methods for speech recognition (language, speech, and communication)* . A Bradford Book .

Johnston, M. D., & Adorf, H.-M. (1992). Scheduling with neural networks: the case of the Hubble space telescope. *Computers & Operations Research* , *19* (3--4), 209-240.

Jurafsky, D., & Martin, J. H. (2000). *Speech and Language Processing: An Introduction to Natural Language Processing, Computational Linguistics, and Speech Recognition* (1 ed.). Upper Saddle River, NJ, USA: Prentice Hall PTR.

Kanal, L. N., & Kumar, V. (1988). *Search in Artificial Intelligence.* Springer.

Kandel, E. R., Schwartz, J. H., & Jessell, T. M. (Eds.). (1991). *Principles of neural science* (3 ed.). Elsevier Science.

Kim, K.-M., Hong, J.-H., & Cho, S.-B. (2007). A semantic Bayesian network approach to retrieving information with intelligent conversational agents. *Information Processing and Management* , 225–236.

Knuth, D. E. (1973). *The Art of computer programming* (2 ed., Vol. 2: Fundamental Algorithms). Ad.

Knuth, D. E., & Moore, R. W. (1975). An analysis of alpha-beta pruning. *AI Jl.* , *6* (4), 293-326.

Kohonen, T. (2000). *Self-Organizing Maps.* Springer .

Konolige, K. (1994). Easy to be hard: Difficult problems for greedy algorithms. In J. Doyle, E. Sandewall, & P. Torasso (Ed.), *KR* (pp. 374-378). Morgan Kaufmann.

Koza, J. R. (1992). *Genetic Programming: On the programming of computers by means of natural selection.* Cambridge, MA, USA: MIT Press.

Koza, J. R., Keane, M. A., Yu, J., Bennet III, F. H., & Mydlowec, W. (2000). Automatic creation of human-competitive programs and controllers by means of genetic programming. *Genetic Programming and Evolvable Machines* , 121-164.

Kröse, B. J., & van der Smagt, P. P. (1993). *An Introduction to neural networks.* Amsterdam: University of Amsterdam.

Kumar, V., Bekey, G. A., Ambrose, R., Lavery, D., Sanderson, D., Yuh, J., et al. (2008). *Robotics: State of the Art and Future Challenges.* Imperial College Press.

Kurzweil, R. (2005). *The Singularity is Near.* Viking.

Laird, J. E., Newell, A., & Rosenbloom, P. S. (1987). SOAR: An Architecture for general intelligence. *Artificial Intelligence* , *33* (1), 1-64.

Langdon, W. B., & Poli, R. (2002). *Foundations of genetic programming.* Springer-Verlag.

LaValle, S. M. (2006). *Planning Algorithms.* Cambridge University Press.

Lindsay, R. K., Feigenbaum, E. A., Buchanan, B. G., & Lederberg, J. (1980). *Applications of artificial intelligence for chemical inference: the Dendral project.* New York: McGraw-Hill.

Livingstone, D. (2006). Turing's Test and believable AI in games. *Computers in Entertainment* , *4* (1).

Loebner. (1991). Retrieved 2015 on 24-November from Home page of the Loebner prize in Artificial Intelligence: http://www.loebner.net/Prizef/loebner-prize.html

Luger, G. (2008). *Artificial Intelligence: Structures and strategies for complex problem solving (6th Edition)*. Pearson.

Manning, C. D., & Schutze, H. (1999). *Foundations of statistical Natural Language Processing*. Cambridge, MA, USA: MIT Press.

Markram, H. (February 2006). The blue brain project. *Nature Reviews Neuroscience* , 153-160 .

McDermott, D. (1978). Planning and acting. *Cognitive Science* , *2* (2), 71-109.

Mendel, G. (1866). über Pflanzen-Hybriden (Experiments on plant hybrids). *Nature Research Society of Brünn* .

Menéndez, Á. L., de Cos Juez, F. J., Lasheras, S., & Álvarez, R. J. (2010). Artificial neural networks applied to cancer detection in a breast screening programme. *Mathematical Models in Medicine, Business & Engineering* , 983–991.

Mihalcea, R., & Strapparava, C. (2006). Learning to laugh (automatically): computational models for humor recognition. *Computational Intelligence* , 126–142.

Miller, G. F., Todd, P. M., & Hegde, S. U. (1989). Designing neural networks using genetic algorithms. In J. D. Schaffer (Ed.), *Proc. of the Third Intl. Conf. on Genetic Algorithms* (pp. 379-384). Arlington, Virginia: Morgan Kaufman.

Moore, E. F. (1959). The shortest path through a maze. *Proc. of the Intl. Symposium on the Theory of Switching, and Annals of the Computation Laboratory of Harvard University* (pp. 285-292). Harvard University Press.

Moravec, H. P. (2000). *Robot: Mere Machine to Transcendent Mind*. New York, NY, USA: Oxford University Press, Inc.

Mueller, E. T. (2006). Chapter 15 - Logics for commonsense reasoning . In E. T. Mueller (Ed.), *Commonsense Reasoning* (pp. 271-298). San Francisco: Morgan Kaufmann.

Murphy, R. R. (2000). *Introduction to AI Robotics* (1st ed.). Cambridge, MA, USA: MIT Press.

Nau, D. S. (1980). Pathology on game trees: A summary of results. *AAAI 80*, (pp. 102-104).

Negnevitsky, M. (2004). *Artificial Intelligence: A guide to intelligent systems* (2nd ed.). Boston, MA, USA: Addison-Wesley.

Newell, A., Shaw, J. C., & Simon, H. A. (1958). Chess-playing programs and the problem of complexity. *IBM Jl. of Research and Development , 2* (4), 320-335.

Nilsson, N. J. (1998). *Artificial Intelligence: A new synthesis*. San Francisco, CA, USA: Morgan Kaufmann Publishers Inc.

Nilsson, N. J. (2005). Human-level Artificial Intelligence? Be serious! *AI Magazine , 26* (4), 68-75.

Nilsson, N. J. (1980). *Principles of Artificial Intelligence*. San Francisco, CA, USA: Morgan Kaufmann Publishers Inc.

Nilsson, N. J. (1971). *Problem-solving methods in Artificial Intelligence*. McGraw-Hill.

Nilsson, N. J. (2009). *The quest for Artificial Intelligence* (1 ed.). New York, NY, USA: Cambridge University Press.

Nsakanda, A. L., Price, W. L., Diaby, M., & Graveld, M. (April 2007). Ensuring population diversity in genetic algorithms: A technical note with application to the cell formation problem. *European Journal of*

Operational Research , 634–638.

Pearl, J. (1984). *Heuristics: Intelligent search strategies for computer problem solving.* Addison-Wesley.

Poli, R., Langdon, W. B., & McPhee, N. F. (2008). *A field guide to genetic programming.* Lulu Enterprises, UK Ltd.

Rabiner, L., & Juang, B.-H. (1993). *Fundamentals of speech recognition.* Upper Saddle River, NJ, USA: Prentice-Hall, Inc.

Rich, E., & Knight, K. (1991). *Artificial Intelligence* (2 ed.). McGraw-Hill.

Rolston, D. W. (1988). *Principles of Artificial Intelligence and Expert Systems Development.* New York, NY, USA: McGraw-Hill, Inc.

Rumelhart, D. E., Hinton, G. E., & Williams, R. J. (1986). Learning representations by back-propagating errors. *Nature* , 533-536 .

Russell, S. J., & Norvig, P. (2009). *Artificial intelligence: A modern approach (3rd edition).* Prentice Hall.

Schalkoff, R. J. (1990). *Artificial Intelligence: An engineering approach.* McGraw-Hill, Inc.

Schmidhuber, J. (2015). Deep learning in neural networks: an overview. *Neural Networks* , 85-117.

Schumaker, R. P., & Chen, H. (2010). Interaction analysis of the ALICE chatterbot: A two-study investigation of dialog and domain questioning. *IEEE Trans. on Systems, Man, and Cybernetics, Part A* , *40* (1), 40-51.

Searle, J. (1990). Is the brain's mind a computer program? *Scientific American* , *262* (1), 26-31.

Searle, J. R. (1994). The rediscovery of the mind. *Jl. of the History of the Behavioral Sciences* , *30* (3), 282-283.

Shortliffe, E. H. (1977). Mycin: A knowledge-based computer program applied to infectious diseases. *Proc. of the Annual Meeting of the Society of Computer Medicine* , 66–69.

Simon, H. A., & Newell, A. (1958). Heuristic problem solving: The next advance in operations research. *Operations Research* , *6*, 1-10.

Singer, P. W. (2009). *Wired for war.* Penguin Books.

Skinner, B. (1953). *Science and human behavior.* Macmillan.

Slagle, J. R. (1971). *Artificial Intelligence: The heuristic programming approach.* McGraw-Hill.

Swingler, K. (1996). *Applying neural networks - a practical guide.* Academic Press.

Thrun, S., Montemerlo, M., Dahlkamp, H., Stavens, D., Aron, A., Diebel, J., et al. (2006). Stanley: The robot that won the DARPA grand challenge: Research articles. *Jl. of Field Robotics* , *23* (9), 661-692.

Turing, A. M. (1950). Computing machinery and intelligence. *Mind* , *LIX(236)*, 433-460.

Ullman, J. D. (1989). *Principles of database and knowledge-base systems.* Computer Science Press.

Urmson, C., & Whittaker, W. (. (2008). Self-Driving Cars and the Urban Challenge. *IEEE Intelligent Systems* , *23* (2), 66-68.

Vinge, V. (1993). The coming technological singularity: How to survive in the post-human era. *Vision-21.*

Waltz, D. L. (1989). The Prospects for Building Truly Intelligent Machines. In S. R. Graubard (Ed.), *The Artificial Intelligence Debate: False Starts, Real Foundations* (pp. 191-212). Cambridge, MA: MIT Press.

Wen, M., Baym, N., Tamuz, O., Teevan, J., Dumais, S., & Kalai, A. (2015). OMG UR funny! Computer-aided humor with an application to chat. *Proc. of The Intl. Conf. on Computational Creativity (ICCC)* .

Wilensky, R. (1983). *Planning and Understanding.* Addison-Wesley.

Wilks, Y. (1975). An intelligent analyzer and understander of English. *Communications of the ACM , 18* (5), 264-274.

Wilks, Y. (1989). *Theoretical issues in natural language processing.* L. Erlbaum.

Winograd, T. (1972). Understanding natural language. *Cognitive Psychology , 3* (1).

Winston, P. H. (1992). *Artificial Intelligence* (3 ed.). Addison-Wesley.

Worzel, W. P., Yub, J., Almal, A. A., & Chinnaiyan, A. M. (February 2009). Applications of genetic programming in cancer research. *The Intl. Jl. of Biochemistry and Cell Biology* , 405–413.

Yoshikawa, T. (1990). *Foundations of robotics: analysis and control.* MIT Press.

Zadeh, L. A. (1965). Fuzzy sets. *Information and Control , 8*, 338-353.

Zimmermann, H.-J. (1991). *Fuzzy set theory---and Its applications* (2 Revised ed.). Kluwer Academic Publishers.

Zweben, M., & Fox, M. (1994). Intelligent scheduling. *User Modeling and User-Adapted Interaction* .

INDEX

ACKNOWLEDGEMENTS

We sincerely thank our family members for their patience and understanding during the creation of this book. Our special thanks to Hira Arshad for the help with illustrations. We thank Tanmoy Chakraborty for his inputs from a student's viewpoint. Thank you to all our faculty reviewers and everyone gave us their honest feedback. We appreciate your continued support.

ADDITIONAL RESOURCES AND MATERIALS

We plan to make additional resources and materials available at:

http://www.cstrends.com/AI

If you have any comments or suggestions for improvement, you may let us know. We really like to hear from you. ai@cstrends.com

ABOUT THE AUTHORS

Binto George is a professor in School of Computer Sciences at Western Illinois University, Macomb, IL, USA. He joined WIU after working at Rutgers University, Newark, NJ. Dr George received his Ph.D. from Indian Institute of Science, Bangalore. Dr George has several publications in Computer Science and has been the principal investigator of National Science Foundation funded curriculum research. He loves teaching and developing new courses. He is committed to making Computer Science accessible to all. Dr. George is a member of the IEEE Computer Science Society and the Association for Computing Machinery.

Gail Carmichael is currently a software developer at Shopify, where she is about to embark on a new and exciting education project. She previously worked as a full-time instructor at Carleton University, where she taught both majors and non-majors a variety of computer science courses. She is particularly passionate about teaching beginners and enticing them to fall in love with computer science, whether as a major or as a tool to help them in their own fields. She co-founded Carleton University's Women in Science and Engineering, helped launch the now Ontario-wide Go Code Girl high school outreach program, and has developed and taught many computing workshops and courses for folks of all ages.

Made in the USA
Middletown, DE
06 July 2017